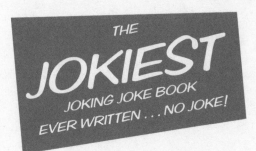

THE

JOKIEST

JOKING JOKE BOOK

EVER WRITTEN . . . NO JOKE!

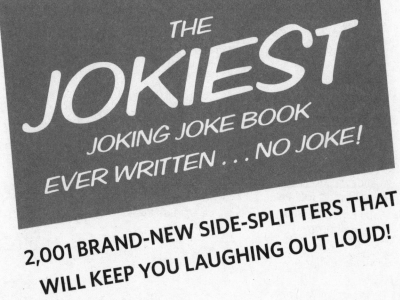

THE JOKIEST
JOKING JOKE BOOK
EVER WRITTEN . . . NO JOKE!

2,001 BRAND-NEW SIDE-SPLITTERS THAT
WILL KEEP YOU LAUGHING OUT LOUD!

Kathi Wagner

ST. MARTIN'S CASTLE POINT
NEW YORK

THE JOKIEST JOKING JOKE BOOK EVER WRITTEN...NO JOKE! Copyright © 2015 by St. Martin's Castle Point. All rights reserved. Printed in the United States of America. For information, address St. Martin's Press, 175 Fifth Avenue, New York, N.Y. 10010.

www.stmartins.com

Design by Phil Mazzone

The Library of Congress Cataloging-in-Publication Data is available upon request.

ISBN 978-1-250-08615-0 (trade paperback)

Our books may be purchased in bulk for promotional, educational, or business use. Please contact your local bookseller or the Macmillan Corporate and Premium Sales Department at 1-800-221-7945, extension 5442, or by e-mail at MacmillanSpecialMarkets@macmillan.com.

First Edition: October 2015

10 9 8 7

To my Dad, who tells the best jokes,

and my Mom, who always listens

CONTENTS

1
JUST KIDDING—Games, Kids, Goats, etc.

What did one sheep say to the other
after being apart a long time?

Why haven't I heard from ewe?

Why did one video game get so mad at the other one?
It was trying to controller.

Why was the deck of cards so sad?
Someone stole their hearts.

Why did the fence like the sheep?
Because it was around them a lot.

How did the playing card dress up?

It wore a suit!

What did the two controllers say when the console's light turned green?
Game on!

How do you know when a goat isn't sure if you are serious?
It asks if you're kidding.

Why did the track shoes up and leave?
They were tired of running around in circles.

What do you get when you put two baby goats together?
Just a couple of kids.

What do you call an upside-down video game?
Game OVER.

Why do cats like to play video games?

Because they have nine lives!

What did the stream name its baby?
Brook.

How do you know when an Xbox has really changed?
It does a 180 instead of a 360.

Why were a tic and a toe losing the fight?
They were missing attack.

Why did the game player have to change his underwear?
They were too titan him.

What do controllers say when the game is over?
Thumbs up!

Why did the tow truck come to the arcade?

One of the games crashed!

Why didn't the troll ever invite the billy goats over?
They could be a little gruff.

How do you know when your computer is not well?
It starts hacking.

Why was the controller so upset with the console?
It was playing games with her.

Why did the Playstation take a staycation?
It was sort of tied down.

How did the football like being the star of the game?
It got a kick out of it.

How did one lightning bolt meet the other?
By striking up a conversation.

How do you know when the moon is starstruck?
It's got a little twinkle in its eye.

Why did Mario have to leave work?
He had a fight with the boss.

How do you know your game is leaving you?
It packed, man.

What do goats do on the Web?
They go trolling.

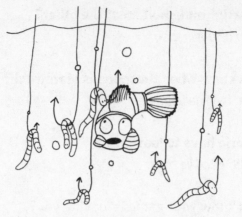

What is Nemo's least favorite game?

Go Fish!

What do gamers order for lunch?
A combo.

What did the video game excel in at track?
The triple jump.

When is it time to feed your video game?
When it starts eyeing the energy bars.

What did the present get for winning the race?
Another ribbon.

What did one gambler say to the other about their odds of winning?
I bet I win.

How did the toilet win the card game?

It had a flush!

How did the square peg fit in the round hole?
He was in bad shape.

Why couldn't the games see each other?
They were back-to-back.

What is a racer's favorite game?
Checkers.

Why couldn't the Tin Man play cards?
He didn't have any hearts.

How did the finger win the game?
It had the most points.

How did the fruits win the card game?
With a pear of aces.

Why did the video game take a break?
It needed a life.

How did the plane win the card game?
It had an ace up its sleeve.

What did the cards do when the poker chip fell down?
They gave him a hand.

How did the video game get its grass cut?
It mode.

What did the police officer say to the game piece?

Don't make a move!

What game do phones like to play?
Ring toss.

What did the rest of the game pieces say to quitting?
No dice.

Where do they put cards for time-out?
In solitary.

What game do new clothes like to play?
Tag.

Why were all the cards looking down in the ground?
There was an ace in the hole.

What do video games always need when they get out of the tub?
Mortals.

What is a train's favorite video game?
Play station.

What did the controllers name their twins?
Plug and Play.

Why did the middle schooler grow up so fast?
Being a teen aged her.

What game do fruits refuse to play?
Fruit basket upset.

What happened when the cupcakes asked the cookies out?

The candy was crushed!

Why was the tree bent over?

It was playing limbo!

Why wouldn't the jacks come out to play?
They had lost their marbles.

Why was the ring covered in thorns?
It was playing ring around the Rosie.

What game are police officers best at?
Cops and robbers.

What game do sharks like to play over lunch?
Name that tuna.

Why was there hay all over the basketball court?
Someone had been playing horse.

What is a game your fingers can never win?
Thumb wrestling.

What's a game you will never forget?
The memory game.

What game can only little eyes play?
I spy.

Which game requires your foot and a toilet?
Kick the can.

What is the game only one ant can win?
King of the hill.

Why was the soda so dizzy?

Someone was playing spin the bottle!

How do you know if your chair likes music?

It was rocking out!

How do boxers kill beetles?
They play slug a bug.

Why wouldn't the rodents go to the party?
Everyone was playing Mouse Trap.

Are you certain the sheep are all getting trimmed?
Yep, it's a shear thing.

Why couldn't the dog or the bird play the game?
It was a game of cat and mouse.

What did the cards say when the poker chips asked if they were coming over?
You bet!

What do Martians play at recess?

Red Rover!

What game do doctors always win?

Operation!

What game feels the guiltiest?

Sorry!

What did one antiperspirant say to the other one about their game?
No sweat.

What did the two cards say about trading suits?
It's a deal.

Why did the controllers decide to go camping?
Their game was in-tents.

What did the sheet music do during the game?
It kept score.

How do screwdrivers play video games?
They take turns.

What game can be very painful to your feet?

Tic-tack-toe!

What did the almond and the pea name their baby?

Peanut!

Why did the video game turn up the heat?
It was freezing.

Why was the elevator the video game champ?
It could reach all the levels.

Why was the flower so happy with its poker game?
It won the pot.

What are ladders the best at in video games?
The extended play.

What do you get when you cross a goat with a horse?
A riding lawnmower.

What do horses say when their feed is all gone?

Hay!

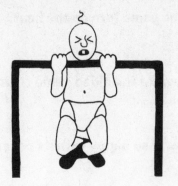

How do toddlers get a workout?

They do pull-ups!

What's a game only toads can play?
Tug of warts.

What is the most fowl game you can play?
Duck, duck, goose.

How was the faucet in such good shape?
It was always running.

What kind of tile did the snake use to decorate its bathroom?
Reptile!

What kind of games do houses play?
Home games.

2
STAR STUDDED—Celebrities, Real Stars, Cowboys, etc.

What is Bruno's favorite planet?
Mars.

Why will John's music be remembered?
Because he's a Legend.

What do you call a fowl kingdom?
A duck dynasty.

Where do Justin and a lumberjack like to go swimming?
In a Timberlake.

What is a star's favorite walk?
On a red carpet.

What's the most talented fish in the ocean?
Starfish.

Why was the actor never down?
He was always acting up.

Why would Tiger Woods make a great sailor?
He's good at staying on course.

What do stars use in their fireplaces?

Holly Wood!

Who named Lady Gaga?
A baby.

What did the feather boa think of the joke?
It was tickled pink.

What movie do elves like to watch?
Gnome Alone.

Why couldn't the famous rapper break a dollar?
Because he was only 50 Cent.

What would Taylor Swift's cat do if she fell in the water?
She would shake it off, off, off.

Why is the villain so good at camping?

Because he's flamous!

What kind of meal does Pharrell order?

A Happy meal!

Where does Ariana like to go on vacation?
To the Grande Canyon.

Of all the golfers, who do you think will go down in history as the best?
Tiger woulds.

Why was Angelina Jolie?
Because it was the holidays.

Why did the boots have to miss the rodeo?
Someone had kicked their heels up.

Why do cowboys wear cowboy boots?
Because it's tough to ride a horse in ski boots.

Why did the cow have to go on a diet?

It was eating like a horse!

How do cowboys rest on the way to the rodeo?

They let the cattle drive!

What does Jennifer Lopez like for dessert?
JLo.

What did the stirrup say to the boot?
Are you spur you want to ride?

How quickly did the stars notice the paparazzi were gone?
In a flash.

What did the Pony Express put on their envelopes?
Stampedes.

Why didn't the cows go into the river?
Because they moo better.

THE JOKIEST JOKING JOKE BOOK EVER WRITTEN . . . NO JOKE!

Why weren't the mountains very hungry?
They had too much desert.

Where do purple dinosaurs live?
In a Barn-ey.

Why wouldn't the cowboy eat his dinner?
They were feeding him grubs.

What did the hunter say that had everyone in the cabin upset?
Bear with me.

Why was the boot so uncomfortable?
He got off on the wrong foot.

What happens when something falls on an actor's head?

She gets starstruck

How did the star know it was in love?

When it fell for another one!

Where did the horse go when he was ready for bed?

He hit the hay.

What do you call a really clumsy shrub?

A fumbleweed!

Which star loves the cold?

Justin B-brrrrr!

How do you get a cowboy to move?
You bronc at them.

Where do cowboys keep their shoes?
In Chuck wagons.

How hard is it for a cowboy to tie a knot in his lasso?
It's a cinch.

What is something even the strongest cowboy can not do?
Hold his horses.

What did the bandits say when the sheriff caught up to them?
Looks like you cactus.

What do celebrities put in their aquariums?

Starfish!

How can you tell when a cowgirl isn't feeling well?
She has cabin fever.

What did one rodeo clown say to the other after the cowboy rode for fifteen minutes?
Howdy do that?

Is it true the rodeo can't go on?
Yep, no bull.

How do cowboys prevent accidents?
They use their saddle horns.

Do cowboys let things get them down?
No, they lariat them go.

Why were the ponies on the carousel?

They were just horsing around!

How much does it cost for a good deer these days?
A buckaroo.

How do cowhands settle who gets the biggest belt and buckle?
By rustling for it.

What is a cowgirl's favorite dressing?
Ranch.

How do you know when a cowboy's really tired?
He has saddlebags under his eyes.

How do cowboys find trouble?
They stirrup some.

How do you fire a cowboy?

You give him the boot!

What did the posse ask as they headed out after the gunslinger?

Are you sheriff you want us to come along?

How can you tell when cowhands are friends?

When they say, "wherever amigo a you go."

How do horses pay for their homes?

In installments.

That happens to horses after they eat?

They get a little hazy.

What did the star always need to make a point?

It was just Sirius.

What do you get when you
mix a Dalmatian with a lamp?

A dog who likes to be in the spotlight!

What do you call a really clumsy shrub?
A fumbleweed.

Why don't birds need to knock?
They just use the buzzard.

Why were lawyers rich in the old West?
There was gold in them there wills.

Why were the cows in so much pain?
They grazed all day.

Why did the ranchers have to use the oven?
They didn't have a range.

What show almost always stands still?
American Idle.

How can you tell when a cowboy's in reverse?
He's back in the saddle.

Why did the mountain go to the movie's premiere?
It wanted a sneak peak.

Why was the machine shed so jealous?
Because the barn danced.

What do you call an overactive cowboy?
A rowdy dudey.

What kind of horses did the young bandits use to ride?
Stickup ponies.

What do you call a lone sailor?
The masted man.

Why did the constellation get into so much trouble?
It was lion.

What did the star tell everyone after the doctor left?
Gemini are having twins!

What would Van Gogh call the Oscars?
A very starry night.

How can you tell if a star is alive?
You check its pulsar.

What is Iggy's favorite flower?
An azalea.

What do you call the star who wants to do it her own way?
Rebel Wilson.

What do stars wear when they go out?
Their evening gowns.

What did everyone think of the lady's new song?
They went Gaga over it.

Why wouldn't the nails leave their post?

They were bent on staying there!

What do you call a movie star in a hot air balloon?

A rising star.

What kind of star is easily deflated?

A pop-star.

Why was there star dust scattered everywhere?

A star burst.

What do you call it when all the stars get together?

An all-star reunion.

Who got blamed when all the buffalo left?

Vamoose did.

What do you get when you cross a dog with a caboose?
A waggin' train.

What did the hyper cowboy's mom tell him to do?
Saddle down.

Why didn't the cowboy answer his mom the 2nd time?
He already herder.

3
VERY TECHNICAL—Computers, Gadgets, etc.

Why was the computer so nervous?

It couldn't get with the program.

Why did the doctor keep checking his TV?

To see if it was operational.

Why didn't the nut like the bolt?

Because he was screwed up.

How do clouds communicate?
They Sky-pe!

How did the bed learn to play piano?
Using sheet music.

What do you call it when a computer gets new shoes?
Rebooted.

What did the computer say when the salesperson asked if they could help?
I'm just browsing.

What happened to the light when the switch was feeling down?
It couldn't go on.

Why did the barn fall down?
It wasn't stable.

Why didn't the computer
Know what to do?

It lost its "memory"

Why were there so many lines between the words?
They were spaced out.

How did the dog get its data back?
It retrieved it.

Why do birds make the best scientists?
They already have their own beakers.

Why did the pen write a circle around the word joke?
It was just joking around.

What is a straw's favorite flower?
Two lips.

How do knights change their TV channels?
With a remoat.

Why was the screw so mad?
Because it didn't get its turn.

Where did the computer and the Internet go when they went out?
On a data.

When do movies do what they are told?
On demand.

Why wouldn't the PC talk about its problems?
It was too personal.

What happens if you give the king of the jungle an Xbox?
You get a lion gamer.

How did the computer monitor describe the keyboard?
Kind of touchy.

How will bees get their packages delivered in the future?
By drones.

Why don't phones wear glasses?
They have contacts.

What is something you should never do to your headphones?
Poke them in their iPhone.

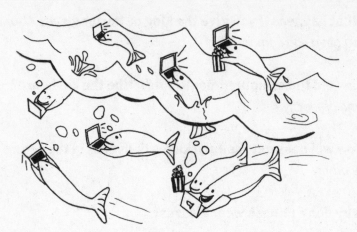

How were the fish able to watch
the latest movie?

They were streaming it!

Why did the coin machine
feel guilty?

Because it broke
a dollar!

What do romantic Twitterers say?

Tweet nothings!

What did the computer do after taking a big breath?
It ex-celled.

How did the smartphone get smarter?
It studied its text books.

How can a phone take pictures without anyone else pushing a button?
All by its selfie.

Why did the chicken want a GPS?
To help it get to the other side of the road.

What do you call a phone that won't share?
Cellfish.

What's an astronaut's favorite key on the computer?

The space bar!

What kind of underwear do lawyers wear?

Legal briefs!

What did one app say to the other app about going on the computer?

Icon if I want to!

Why was the computer always happy?

It had a really good Outlook.

Why did it take so long for the laptop to get in the door?

It was trying all of its keys.

What did the computer ask the tech?

How about you get with the program?

How do candles get together on the Web?

They use their wikis.

Why did the stove always get mad?

It was hot-tempered!

What is a shark's favorite type of technology?
Bluetooth.

How did the fence share its favorite moments?
By posting them.

How did the disc put on its makeup?
It used its compact.

What do you get when you cross a battery and a zombie?
A battery that will never die.

How do clocks communicate?
They tick-tock to each other.

What video game do pigs like to play in the car?

Wii wii wii all the way home!

Why did the pens decide to become friends?
They just clicked.

Why did the computer set a trap?
It had a mouse.

What did the e-mail tell the document?
All good things come to a send!

How did one mouse feel about the other mouse finding the cheese?
It was amazed.

What did the speakers say to the TV that made it nervous?
You're surrounded!

How do you know a computer needs glasses?

It has trouble seeing the sites!

How do trees sign off of their computers?
They log out.

How would you talk to Santa if he were a computer?
You would sit on his laptop.

Which fish did the computer pick for a pet?
The betta.

Why did the exterminator have to spray the computer?
He had to debug it.

Why did the computer like tennis?
It was a good server.

Why did the smoke detector have to go?
It wasn't very alert.

What did the projector say as its bulb was being replaced?
But the show must go on.

What do you call it when a picture goes to the mall?
Photo shopping.

What is a computer's favorite part of art class?
The cutting and pasting.

Why did the sand turn into glass?
It wanted to make a spectacle of itself.

Why did the notebook need glasses?

It couldn't read between the lines!

Why couldn't anyone get the computer open?
It was all locked up.

Why don't bugs need cable to watch TV?
They have their own antennas.

What was the sports camera's only dream?
To go pro.

Why was the money off by itself in the bank?
It was all a-loan.

Where do TV's like to go on vacation?
To remote places.

Why was the corn so good at music?
It could play by ear.

What do you do with an upset Web site?
You com it down.

How can a computer see the world?
Through its Windows.

How does a clock put its gloves on?
One hand at a time.

Why didn't the toys want to go to the party?
The batteries weren't included.

How did the caveman let his friends
know what he was doing?

He posted it on his wall!

Why does every pair of pants look different?
They all have different genes.

Why was the clock so mad at the marker?
It had written all over its face.

What did the recorder tell the microphone?
You can say that again.

What did the Web site ask the mouse?
Can you take me home?

How do you know when a balloon comes in unannounced?
When it bursts into the room.

Why did the piggy bank need to be fixed?

It was broke!

How do you know when your screwdriver is sick?
It takes a turn for the worse.

How did the Instagram account know someone was there?
They were following him.

Where does the world's biggest spider live?
In the World Wide Web.

How do birds communicate?
They tweet.

Why did someone keep dropping the flash drives?
They were all thumbs.

What do you get when you
cross earphones and a flower?

Ear buds!

What do you get when you combine a cow with the Internet?
Some milk and a bunch of cookies.

How does a DVD player get from place to place?
It lets the disc drive.

What is the fastest cracker in the box?
An Instagraham.

Where do e-mails like to play?
In their sent box.

What do you feed your big screen?
A TV dinner.

4
AROUND THE HOUSE—
Household Items, Yards, etc.

What has several keys, numerous windows, and even a mouse but isn't a house?
A computer.

Why did the sewing machine always look busy?
Because that's how it seams.

Why did the couch jump in front of the falling lamp?
To cushion its fall.

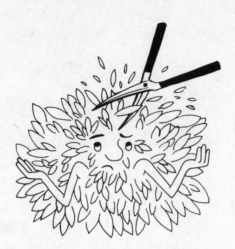

How did the bush get over being trimmed?

It shrubbed it off!

Why was the soap so mad?

The washcloth rubbed it the wrong way!

What do you call it when one step sues another step?
A stair case.

What do you get when you put your pants on a diet?
Skinny jeans.

What did the windows say to the blinds as they were going away?
I guess it's curtains for us!

What do you call a basement light that won't work?
Down and out.

Why did the stairs have to keep checking the instructions?
Somehow it took the wrong steps.

What are the softest type of crimes to solve?
Pillow cases.

What kind of shoes do sinks hate the most?
Clogs.

How will things turn out for the radio in the future?
Stay tuned.

What was the burglar doing in the bank?
Trying to find a safe place.

How do steps like to compete?
By having stairing contests.

THE JOKIEST JOKING JOKE BOOK EVER WRITTEN . . . NO JOKE!

Why did the toilet turn so red?
It was flushed.

What goes undercover but isn't a spy?
Your pajamas.

Why couldn't the TV buy anything?
Because it was flat broke.

What did one flashlight tell the other?
Come ON!

What did the ice do even though someone left the freezer open?
It kept its cool.

What kind of nail should you
never hit with a hammer?

Your fingernail!

What did the drill say at the end of its life?

I sure have been through a lot.

How can you tell when a washing machine is resting?

It takes a load off.

How can you tell when a door isn't going to change its mind?

When it is completely closed to it.

What did the father mower tell his son when life got really hard?

When the mowing gets tough, the tough get mowing!

Why was the picture innocent?

Because it was framed.

What did the angry shoes say to the sock?
You stink!

How do you know when your dishes are through?
They are all washed up.

Why did the rug need a haircut?
Because it was shaggy.

How can you tell when a bell was in an accident?
It has a ding in it.

What do houses call chores?
Homework.

What do windows do when it's sunny outside?

Put on their shades!

What did the washing
machine do when it quit?

It unloaded!

How did the blinds know the windows were lying?
They could see right through them.

Why was the paint all mixed up?
It was really shaken.

What do you call it when two toys go out together?
A play date.

Why was the window sill so nervous?
It was a little on the ledge.

Why did the washcloth silence the phone?
It was all wrung out.

What did the cupboard's and cabinet's baby look like?
A-door-able.

How did the door do in basketball?
He got a slam-dunk!

What did the mother pen tell her baby?
If you want something done write, you have to do it yourself.

What did one bolt tell the other?
You're nuts!

What did one piece of lumber say to the other piece of lumber?
I'm board.

What is the doll's favorite way to cook?

Barbie-Q!

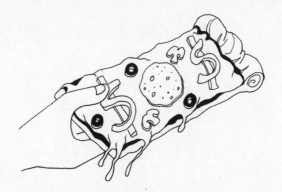

What do you call money that
you buy pizza with?

Pizza dough!

What did the hook say to the towel?
Hang in there!

What did the wood tell the varnish?
I'm finished.

Why did the knife have to leave the kitchen?
It just couldn't cut it.

What was wrong with the kitchen sink?
It was really drained!

Why couldn't the pool table go on with the game?
It didn't have a cue.

Why are jeans always sad?

Because they're blue!

What do mice build their houses out of?
Brick of cheese.

How do itches bake their cakes?
From scratch.

How did the toy car get to the toy store?
It went around the block.

What piece of furniture is the most laid-back?
The recliner.

Why couldn't the dryer trust the washing machine?
Sometimes it was a little wishy-washy.

What sounds clean,
but gets dirtier as you use it?

A washcloth!

Why was the ladder broken?
It over extended itself.

How do you dress a door?
You clothes it.

Why weren't the stairs in charge anymore?
They stepped down.

Why was the door so sticky?
Because of the jam.

How did the recliner move after it broke its leg?
Very chairfully.

Why did the firefighters think they
should have been invited to the party?

It was a house warming!

How can you tell when your teddy bear has a cold?
It's all stuffed up.

What did the candle say when it didn't smell anymore?
Scents when?

Who knew the house the best?
The door knew it both inside and out.

Did the dresser like the socks?
Sort of.

Why was the nurse worried about her oven?
It had a temperature.

How did the lid help the dish?
She covered him.

Where did the snake lose its skin?
In the shed.

Why was the party all wet?
It was a shower.

What did the toilet paper do when it reached the end?
It rolled with it.

What's the biggest moment in a stair's life?
Its first step.

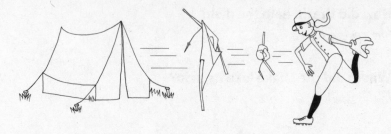

What do you get when you combine
baseball and camping?

You pitch a tent!

What did the hurdler do when she lost the race?
She got over it.

What did the window do for the frame?
It looked out for it.

Why did the window call the doctor?
Because it was in pane.

Why was the shoe so quiet?
It bit its tongue.

How did the argument between the shirt and the wrinkles end?
They ironed it out.

How did the yard get so much money?

It raked it in!

How do you fix a broken mallard?
With duct tape.

How did they know the bone was in trouble?
It was in the doghouse.

What happened when someone dropped the baby's toy?
It got a little rattled.

What kind of conversation did the mattress and the bed-spread have?
Pillow talk.

Why was the sink so unhappy with the scrubber?
It was sponging off of everyone.

Why was the beater so dizzy?
They were trying to mixer up.

How do you catch a jacket?
With a coat hook.

What happened when the dryer fell?
It took a tumble.

What did the dirty laundry do after it was washed?
It hung around.

THE JOKIEST JOKING JOKE BOOK EVER WRITTEN . . . NO JOKE!

What did the demolition crew say about the building?

It's going down.

How did the firefighter become chief?

He climbed the ladder.

Why wasn't the shirt tucked in?

It was just hanging out.

How did the shopping bag get torn?
It was malled.

What did the bathtub give the shower when they got engaged?
A ring.

What happened when the two combs got into a fight?
They parted ways.

How did the water feel about going underground?
It didn't take it well.

What did the baby comb say to the big comb when they bumped into each other?
I'm fine.

THE JOKIEST JOKING JOKE BOOK EVER WRITTEN . . . NO JOKE!

What did the thread tell the needle?
Just sew you know, I'm a little tied up.

What did the mother toilet do when the baby toilet wouldn't quit talking?
She put a lid on it.

What did the firefighter think about the fire?
That it was alarming.

What did the concrete blocks do when they met?
Cemented their friendship.

What does a Yes person say all the time?
I don't "no."

What do you call two straws
that grew up together?

Sip-lings!

What did the broom do to the yard stick?

Swept it off its feet!

Why didn't the motel go out?
It decided to stay inn.

What did they call the rope's sense of humor?
A little twisted.

How did the soda slide under the door?
It was flat.

Who is always very timely?
Your alarm.

What did one alarm clock say to the other alarm clock?
Do you ever hear a ringing in your ears?

How did the chicken react to the joke?
It was a good egg about it.

What would you call it if you sat down on a chewed piece of gum?
A very sticky situation.

Why do doors like nighttime best?
They're knockturnal.

Why did the money seem so different to everyone?
It had changed.

What happened when Santa got the flu?
He made his-elf sick.

Why was the horse laughing?

It was told to giddy-up!

How did the shoes find their missing laces?
They ran them down.

Why didn't the bread ever rise?
There was no knead.

What is the favorite game for potatoes and hamburger?
Hash tag.

Why should you always ask for your mother's permission first?
Because your father no's best.

What did the watch say to the scale?
Weight a minute!

Why were the puzzle pieces having a party?

They wanted to get together!

What did the pliers do for the drill?

They helped him out a bit.

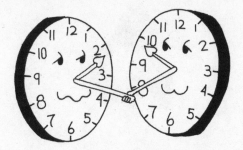

How can you tell when two
clocks like each other?

They're holding hands!

Why don't penguins ever get married?
They get cold feet.

What did the glasses say to the eyes?
Made you look!

What did the owls say when the hawks caught them trying to imitate them?
Hawkward!

What did the shirt say to the talkative pair of jeans?
Zip it!

What do you say to a pizza when you want to take its picture?
Cheese!

What's black and white and red all over?

A penguin with a rash!

Why was the sweater so organized?
It was always buttoned up.

Why is anger so popular now?
It's all the rage.

What did Mrs. Corn do when she found out Mr. Corn was canned?
She gave him an ear full.

What did the one mad washcloth tell the other?
You just wait towel I tell mom!

What do you call it when two bats fight?
A battle.

What choice did the cord give the battery?
Adaptor else.

Why didn't the car ask the driveway out?
It wasn't very approachable.

What did the muscles say to the dumbbells?
Give me strength.

What do you call a small firecracker?
A baby boomer.

What were the foods so worried about?
That you are what eats you.

Why was the fish laughing so hard at the fisherman holding the shoe?
Because he was off the hook.

What is it called when two mountains meet?
A summit.

How did the store get rid of the slow-moving items?
They seldom.

How do mountains say no?
They decline.

What do you call a young note?
A minor.

Who's the boss in a family?
Isn't it apparent?

How did the doctor get better at his shots?
With a lot of practice.

Why did the doctor have to see the tree?
It broke a limb.

Why did the dock think it needed to change?
Because of the pier's pressure.

Why wouldn't the fingernail get up?
It wanted to stay in its bed.

What would Elsa's baby look like if she had one?

Snow cute!

How do you know when a door agrees with you?
It knobs its head.

How does a porcupine stay warm in the winter?
It goes under its quilts.

Why was the Easter egg so nervous?
Someone was hunting it.

What did the teddy bear say to the polar bear?
Is this fur real?

Why didn't the flower need its family as much?
It was all grown up.

Why couldn't the flower ride the bike?

Its pedals fell off.

What did one knife say to the other when it was bugging him?

Cut it out.

What do you get when you mix an owl with a nurse?

Who cares?

Why was the hair so good in the play?

It knew its part.

What did the doctor ask the dumbbells?

Have you been weighting long?

What did the heart, the kidneys, and the liver do right before their trip?

They got organized!

What part of the store can you tell
someone exactly how you feel?

The express lane!

What did the butter say to the jam?

I'm on a roll.

What kind of dog has the strongest punch?

A boxer.

How do dogs argue with each other?

They beg to differ.

What did the ruler tell the doctor?

Give it to me straight.

What did one candy bar say to the other?

What's eating you?

What did one tree ask the other right before vacation?
When do we leave?

What did the cake say to the party hat?
I need a favor.

How did the rumor get started about someone taking the cake?
The frosting spread it.

How come nobody wanted to play with the jaguar?
Because it was a cheetah!

How did the mother dalmatian find her baby?
She spotted it.

Why was the rope trying to be brave?

It didn't want to be a-frayed!

Why did the zipper get stuck?
It got caught in a flytrap.

What do you get when you see One Direction three times?
3D.

What did the pasta say when it was playing hide and seek?
Spaghetti or not, here I come.

What do you get when you put a kitten on a scanner?
A copycat.

What do you get when you combine honey with a comb?
Very sticky hair.

Did the gloves win the contest?
Hands down!

How can you tell when your scissors get mad?

They're a little snippy!

What comes between before school and after school?
Middle school.

Why couldn't the crayon see anything?
It blacked out!

Why was the ruler so confused?
It couldn't think straight.

What did one ruler say when the other ruler was leaving?
So long!

What do you call it when there's nothing on your math homework?
No problem.

Why couldn't the second class of kids get on the plane?
They only had room for the first class.

Why were the scissors smiling?
Because they had their work cut out for them.

Why did the red marker get in trouble for writing in the book?
Because it red it all by itself.

What are the best steps to take to solve a really hard math problem?

The steps up to your teacher's desk.

Why was the dot-to-dot struggling?

It couldn't seem to connect.

What's another name for counterfeit money?

Play dough.

Why did the newspaper struggle in school?

It was having trouble with its Times tables.

What do you call a thermometer that doesn't pass its test?

A failed a-temp.

Why did the cowboy have to leave school?

For horsing around too much!

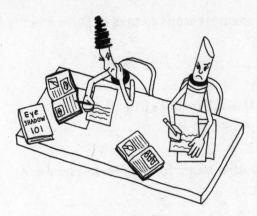

Why did the lipstick and mascara
have to stay after school?

To do makeup work!

What did the snowman learn about?

Numb brrrrs!

What do you call dirt that isn't real?
Play ground.

How did the cars do in school?
They didn't pass.

Why did the sheet music do well on a test?
It had taken notes.

How did the eagle do in school?
It soared.

How did the rainbow do in school?
It passed with flying colors.

How did the carpenters do in school?
They finished.

How did the boat do in school?
It sailed through.

How did the road do at coloring?
It stayed inside the lines.

What did the bookshelves do at school?
They learned their upper and lower cases.

How did the shovel do in school?
It ditched a few classes.

What did the baggie do when the teacher told him no more talking?

He zipped it up!

Why couldn't the ice cream give a speech?

Because it froze!

Which part of school is a farmer's favorite?
Field trips.

How did the computer programs do in school?
They excelled.

How was school for the traffic light?
A little stop and go.

How was school for the concrete?
Really hard.

Why couldn't Humpty Dumpty wait for winter?
Because he had a great fall.

How did Bob the Builder do in school?
He nailed it.

What's a lawyer's favorite part of school?
Recess.

How did the fireman do in school?
Smoking.

What did one pencil say to the other?
You have a good point!

How did the king do in school?
He liked his subjects.

How did the phone do in school?

It got called on a lot for the answers!

Why did the bicycle do poorly in school?
He was two tired.

Why did the tennis player help the lunch lady?
He loved to serve.

Why was the tongue so special?
It stuck out.

How did the egg do in class?
It was a Grade-A student.

How did the music do in school?
Noteworthy.

Why did the giant have to stay after school?

He was in big trouble!

Why did the cafeteria flunk school?
It was always out to lunch.

Why did the doctors do well in school?
They gave it their best shot.

How come the football player is bad in art class?
He always tackles his projects.

How did the dancer do in class?
She tapped lightly around the subjects.

What was the beaker's favorite part of school?
That it graduated.

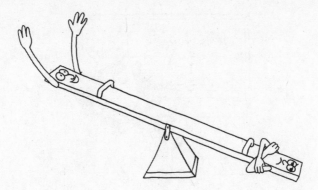

How did the seesaw feel from time to time?

It had its ups and downs!

How did the cat do in school?
Purrfect, because it was the teacher's pet.

Why did the hopscotch get in trouble?
It skipped class.

What was the movie's favorite part in school?
Extra credits.

How did the panda do in school?
It bearly made it.

How did the basketball do in school?
Slam dunk.

Why did the apple have to stay after school?

It was fresh!

How did Pacman like his classes?
He ate them up.

How did the apple do in school?
It was the teacher's favorite.

How come no one ate the cookies in the cafeteria?
Because they were crumby.

Why did the empty piggy bank flunk class?
Because he couldn't pay attention.

How did the candy do in school?
It fudged on its exam.

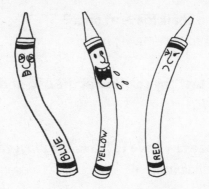

Which color is the loudest?

Yellow!

How did the history book do in school?

It past.

What kind of math do fish do in their schools?

Algaebra!

Why did all the chalk leave at once?
They went back to the drawing board.

What did one test say to other at the end of the day?
And that's final!

Why did the seesaw have to leave the playground?
It was a little unbalanced.

How do you know when a dog is bossy?
It barks orders.

Why did the chalk fall asleep in class?
It was really board.

How did the dog get through school?

It asked for yelp!

Why was the exam in a bad mood?

It was feeling a little testy!

What kind of paint do you use to paint a hand?
Finger paint!

Where do teachers live?
In school houses.

How long is a dollar's school year?
Four quarters.

Where do planks learn everything they need to know?
At boarding school.

When do owls learn the most?
At night school.

How did the baseball players do in school?

They knocked it out of the park!

What was the thermometer doing in school?
Getting its degree.

Why did they build onto the school cafeteria?
To give the lunch room.

What part of your eye goes to school?
Your pupil.

Why was the jump rope in timeout?
It skipped class.

Why are schools so full of energy?
They have a lot of pep rallies.

What did the doughnuts think about school?

They liked the hole thing!

How did the wand do at magic school?
He was a wizard at it.

How did the test disappear?
A student took it.

What do fish practice at their piano lessons?
Their scales.

Why was the finger in trouble?
For poking fun.

Why was the shoe late?
It was a little tied up.

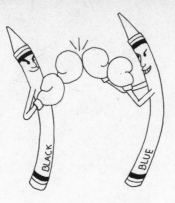

Which two colors hurt the most?

Black and blue!

Where do little plants go to learn?
Nursery schools.

Where do pens sleep?
Under sheets of paper.

Why didn't the rope show up to its exercise class?
It decided to skip it.

Why did the rotten milk always want more stuff?
It was spoiled.

Why did the brain get in trouble in school?
It was thinking out loud.

Why did the fish stay home from school?
It was feeling eel.

Knock, knock. Who's there? I'm kinda. I'm kinda who?

I'm kinda tired of knocking, can I come in?

Knock, knock. Who's there? Justin. Justin who?

Justin time to see you.

Knock, knock. Who's there? Can I. Can I who?

Can I just ring your bell the next time?

Knock, knock. Who's there? Ima. Ima who?

Ima gonna go if you don't open the door.

Knock, knock. Who's there? Don't Chew. Don't chew who?

Don't chew want the pizza that you ordered?

Knock, knock. Who's there? Eye. Eye who?

Eye wish the ice cream truck would come by.

Knock, knock. Who's there? Nose. Nose who?

Nose anybody who wants a puppy?

Knock, knock. Who's there? Ear. Ear who? Ear that?

I think someone is here.

Knock, knock. Who's there? Necks. Necks who?

Necks time I come to the door I'll ring.

Knock, knock. Who's there? Sea. Sea who?
Sea you at the beach.

Knock, knock. Who's there? Hair. Hair who?
Hair I am!

Knock, knock. Who's there? Sneaker. Sneaker who?
Sneaker in the back door.

Knock, knock. Who's there? Hand. Hand who?
Hand over the pizza.

Knock, knock. Who's there? Boy. Boy who?
Boy it's nice out here.

Knock, knock. Who's there? Woody. Woody who?
Woody like to come out and play ball with me?

Knock, knock. Who's there? Connie. Connie who?
Connie come out and play?

Knock, knock. Who's there? Blue. Blue who?
Blue you, I'm sad.

Knock, knock. Who's there? Sky. Sky who?
Sky was wondering if you want to look at the stars?

Knock, knock. Who's there?
Ben here before.

Knock, knock. Who's there?
Wheat a minute, I'll be right in

Knock, knock. Who's there?
Later, gator; I'm leaving.

Knock, knock. Who's there?
Cheetah, you were supposed to be hiding outside.

Knock, knock. Who's there? Rhino. Rhino who?
Rhino who you are.

Knock, knock. Who's there? Owl. Owl who?
Owl have to check.

there? Schooner. Schooner who?

u have to come out.

k. Who's there? Howie. Howie who?

nna get in if you don't open the door?

ock, knock. Who's there? Winter. Winter who?

Winter you going to decide?

Knock, knock. Who's there? Surprise. Surprise who?
Surprise, it's your birthday!

Knock, knock. Who's there? Wreath. Wreath who?
Wreath me alone, I'm mad.

Knock, knock. Who's there? Justin. Justin who?
Justin time, it's starting to rain.

Knock, knock. Who's there? Linda. Linda who?
Linda me a hand, this box is heavy.

Knock, knock. Who's there? Ima. Ima who?
Ima fraid so please let me in.

Knock, knock. Who's there? Izza. Izza who?
Izza anybody home?

Knock, knock. Who's there? Tag. Tag who?
Tag, you're it!

Knock, knock. Who's there? Ida. Ida who?
Ida called, but I wanted to see you.

Knock, knock. Who's there? Shirley. Shirley who?
Shirley you know who I am.

Knock, knock. Who's there? Whoo. Whoo who?
Whoo hooo, let's have a party!

Knock, knock. Who's there? Olive. Olive who?
Olive us.

Knock, knock. Who's there? Door bell. Door bell who?
Door bell repair person.

Knock, knock. Who's there? Dewey. Dewey who?

Dewey have to keep knocking?

Knock, knock. Who's there? Candace. Candace who?

Candace be real or are we dreaming?

Knock, knock. Who's there? Cara. Cara who?

Cara if I stay for lunch?

Knock, knock. Who's there? Doris. Doris who?

Doris open, do you want me to close it?

Knock, knock. Who's there? Elsa. Elsa who?

Elsa you open this door or I'm leaving.

Knock, knock. Who's there? Eileen. Eileen who?

Eileen on the door, but it still won't open.

Knock, knock. Who's there? Why. Why who?
Why aren't you answering?

Knock, knock. Who's there? Abby. Abby who?
Abby right back, I forgot something.

Knock, knock. Who's there? Ivan. Ivan who?
Ivan standing out here way too long.

Knock, knock. Who's there? Simon. Simon who?
Simon says open the door.

Knock, knock. Who's there? Hope. Hope who?
Hope you don't mind me stopping by.

Knock, knock. Who's there? Isabelle. Isabelle who?
Isabelle broken?

Knock, knock. Who's there? Iva. Iva who?

Iva had enough of you.

Knock, knock. Who's there? Dora. Dora who?

Dora was already open.

Knock, knock. Who's there? Harriet. Harriet who?

Harriet all the birthday cake.

Knock, knock. Who's there? Gwen. Gwen who?

Gwen are we going to play something other than this door game?

Knock, knock. Who's there? Heidi. Heidi who?

Heidi go seek and you're it!

Knock, knock. Who's there? Santa. Santa who?

Santa who can't get down the chimney.

Knock, knock. Who's there? Wyatt. Wyatt who?

Wyatt this house and not yours?

Knock, knock. Who's there? Ima. Ima who?

Ima cold, let me in!

Knock, knock. Who's there? I van. I van who?

I van all over town looking for you.

Knock, knock. Who's there? Vincent. Vincent who?

Vincent me here to get you.

Knock, knock. Who's there? Preston. Preston who?

Preston your bell but it didn't ring.

Knock, knock. Who's there? Paul. Paul who?

Paul I do is knock all day long.

Knock, knock. Who's there? Ivan. Ivan who?
Ivan thinking about you!

Knock, knock. Who's there? Heywood. Heywood who?
Heywood you mind if I borrow some sugar?

Knock, knock. Who's there? Hans. Hans who?
Hans down, you have the nicest house.

Knock, knock. Who's there? Holly. Holly who?
Hollywood's calling, gotta run!

Knock, knock. Who's there? Garrett. Garrett who?
Garrett all if I swing on your porch?

Knock, knock. Who's there? Ezra. Ezra who?
Ezra anybody else home?

Knock, knock. Who's there? Tommy. Tommy who?
Tommy this is just another house.

Knock, knock. Who's there? Tyne. Tyne who?
Tyne for you to come out and play.

Knock, knock. Who's there? Shelly. Shelly who?
Shelly come back some other time.

Knock, knock. Who's there? Cher. Cher who?
Cher my candy with me?

Knock, knock. Who's there? Sari. Sari who?
Sari for waking you up.

Knock, knock. Who's there? Penny. Penny who?
Penny chance you might open the door?

Knock, knock. Who's there? Ken. Ken who?

Ken I use your bathroom?

Knock, knock. Who's there? Bettie. Bettie who?

Bettie you thought it was someone else.

Knock, knock. Who's there? Reuben. Reuben who?

Reuben gone a long time.

Knock, knock. Who's there? Kenna. Kenna who?

Kenna talk to you for a minute?

Knock, Knock. Who's There? Barry. Barry who?

It's Barry dark out here, can you turn on the light?

What do you call it when you have brain surgery?

Being open-minded!

What happens when a football team pays too much during a draft?

They get a quarter back.

How do you stop two bats from hitting each other?

Put them in the calm-bat zone.

What did the police officer say to the roller coaster after it came speeding by?

Looks like I'm gonna have to take you for a ride!

How did the bowling ball get into an accident?
By changing lanes.

Why was the clock always late?
It was broken.

How did the detective catch the necklace thief?
Because of the chain of events.

Why did one baseball break up with the other baseball?
They were threw.

Is there anything worse than competing against three professional golfers?
Yes, fore.

Why was the gum so sad?

He got chewed out!

How come a baseball has
such a great sense of humor?

It's always in stitches!

What's a golfer's favorite sandwich?
A club.

How did the golfer know he was going to win the game?
A birdie told him.

Why didn't the baseball glove get the flu?
It wasn't catchable.

Where does a down-and-out bowling ball go?
The gutter.

Why didn't the phone answer a lot of the time?
It was disconnected.

What did the phone say at the end of a bad connection?
We're breaking up!

Why did the fisherman hang up on his friend?
Because he had a fish on the other line.

What sport should you be in if you are always mad?
Cross-country.

Why did one phone break up with the other phone?
Because he had too many hang-ups?

Why did everyone think the necklace looked suspicious?
It had bead-y eyes.

THE JOKIEST JOKING JOKE BOOK EVER WRITTEN . . . NO JOKE!

What kind of underwear is the toughest?

Boxers!

Why wouldn't the shirt leave the hanger alone?
It was hung up on it.

Who did the slowest skier beat in the race?

Snowbody!

Why did the football coach cut the clock in half?
It was halftime.

Why was the nose such a bad basketball player?
Because it didn't like to be picked.

How do you catch a volleyball fish?
With a volleyball net.

What's the best way to keep your phone dry?
Wring it out.

Why was the closet pole so mad at the hangers?
They all hung up on him.

What did the camera tell the distracted lens?

FOCUS!

Why can't you play baseball with a burglar?

Because he always steals home!

How did the basketball team know their player was sick?
He threw up.

Why did the boxer get kicked out of the pool?
For being on the ropes.

Why was the health instructor let go?
Because it was a bad fit.

When did the giants know they had made it?
When they were in the big leagues.

What kind of phones do they use in prison?
Cell phones.

What do you call a ball's messy room?

A ball pit!

Why do doctors need phones?
So they can call the shots.

What wouldn't one phone talk to the other phone?
Because it was busy.

Why wasn't the baseball allowed to leave the park?
Because it was grounded.

How did the phone feel about the referee's opinion?
It was a good call.

What do you get when you blend a basketball star and a poet?
Someone who plays in the prose.

How do you propose to a ball field?
With a diamond.

What did the clothes do when the pins called?
They stayed on the line.

Which punctuation mark is the fastest?
The dash.

How did the music do in sports?
It scored.

What was the bulldozer doing at the baseball diamond?
Leveling out the playing field.

What kind of trash do cats make?

Kitty litter!

How do barbarians play ball?
They tend to overthrow.

What happened when all the appliances played baseball?
The dishwasher was safe.

What do golfers always wear to their games?
Their Tee-shirts.

Why was one phone not so sure about the other one?
It was acting a little phony.

How did the track celebrate its big moment?
It had a field day.

How did the camera blow up the phone?

With a photobomb!

Why did the skier give up skiing?
He was snow board.

What do you call it when two phones almost run into each other?
A close call.

What do you get when you combine a baby bird and a laptop?
A computer that tweets by itself.

How do you know when electricity is in trouble?
It gets grounded.

Why was the medicine always in trouble?
For being such a pill.

What is a bird's favorite part of football?

The tailgate parties!

Why was the batter sent to the dugout?
He couldn't get the swing of it.

What happened when the baseball got hit?
It bawled.

How did the soccer players get so far?
They set lots of goals for themselves.

How did the ball player sneak past second base?
He kept very steal.

Why were the golfers all scratched up?
The course was coarse.

 THE JOKIEST JOKING JOKE BOOK EVER WRITTEN . . . NO JOKE!

Why did the golf club get his license?
Because he was an excellent driver.

What is a golfer's least favorite part of their underwear?
The wedge.

Did the golfer play an extra round?
Of course.

What did the owl say when it answered its cell?
Whooo's calling?

How long did the longest game of golf take?
Fore ever.

Where does a shovel sit at a ball game?
In the dugout.

What did the baseball say at the end of the game?
I am threw!

Why did the paint have to buy new shoes?
Sometimes it ran.

How do you make a baseball cake?
With baseball batter.

Who does the phone's hair?
Its stylus.

How can you tell when the
radio was in no mood to joke?

It's Sirius!

Why didn't the
zombie answer
its call?

It was in the
dead zone!

How come the phone never had a girlfriend?
It was always breaking up.

What did the phone and the tower have?
A long-distance relationship.

What do worn-out phones do when they retire?
They hang it up.

Why didn't the phone recognize a number?
It didn't ring a bell.

Why did the softball leave the game?
Someone decided to play hardball.

Why didn't the window answer the phone?

It screened its calls!

What did one canoe say to the other?
Kayak you a question?

What did the runners do when the track was closed?
They took it in stride.

What happened after the racecar driver hurt himself?
He made a speedy recovery.

How do you get an uncooperative racecar to the track?
You drag it.

How did the golfer sink a boat?
He had a hole in one.

Why did the phone get an A on its test?

Because it was a smart phone!

How did the ballerina get a head of the rest?
She was on her toes.

Why was the baseball in love with the bat?
It was a real knockout.

Why did the soccer ball leave the game?
It came apart at the seams.

Where do the mountains like to drive?
The driving range.

Where did the golf club go to celebrate?
To a golf ball.

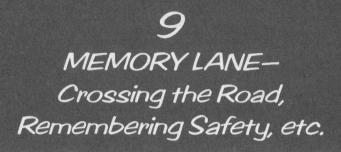

9
MEMORY LANE—
Crossing the Road,
Remembering Safety, etc.

Why couldn't the tree answer the question?

He was stumped!

What did Good Cop have after Lord Business erased his face?
A Blank look.

What do you call it when a tank can't stop?
Un-brake-able.

How did Mator know he needed a change?
He was stuck in a rut.

Where do frogs like to store all their stuff?

On their iPads!

What do you call a truck that wears a size 13 shoe?
Big Foot.

How you keep your pants from falling off their seat?
You belt them in.

Why did the semi have to pull over to sleep?
It was very tire-d.

When can a highway have problems?
When it gets out of line.

Why did the concrete fail the first time?
It didn't try hard enough.

What did the turn signal do
when he couldn't turn right?

He left!

How did the intersection feel about all of the traffic?
Very cross.

Why was the trailer rolling away?
It went off without its hitch.

What did one ear ask the other when they reached the intersection?
Where do we go from hear?

Why did the construction hats have to be apart?
They couldn't work it out.

Where do cars go on vacation?
Cruises.

What did the muffler say after the long trip?

I'm exhaust-ed!

What do you get when you combine a pickup and thunder?
A Big Boom truck.

Why did the construction cone get squashed?

It was in the zone!

Why did the turn signal miss the turn?
It blinked.

What do you call racing 24/7?
Life in the fast lane.

What do you call it when your hatchet hits your car?
An axe-i-dent.

How do you know when a tire is well?
It's not slick.

What did the bowling balls do when the lane closed?
They rolled with it.

How did the concrete feel about leaving the blocks?
It was very hard!

Why was the CAUTION sign so smart?
It was SLOW to anger.

What game really messes up traffic?
Red light, green light, red light . . .

What do you call an army officer who crashes his car?
Captain Crunch.

What did the radio say to the GPS?
I'll follow you anywhere.

THE JOKIEST JOKING JOKE BOOK EVER WRITTEN . . . NO JOKE!

What sometimes slows down construction?

Building BLOCKS!

Why did the racecar quit altogether?
It was a drag.

How did the car improve its driving?
It took a crash course.

What do you have when you have two people named Lane on the same road?
A two-Lane highway.

Why were the plants so nervous when the flower drove?
It always put the petal to the metal.

How did the mechanic get the cars to wait for him?
He stalled them.

Why was the racecar so weak?

It had been fasting for too long.

How did the two trucks survive in the wilderness?

They fendered for themselves.

Why wouldn't the wrenches let the screwdrivers ride with them?

They were backseat drivers.

Why couldn't the cars go anywhere?

Someone borrowed their wheels.

How do you know when a camera is moving really fast?

It zooms.

When is a dirty room better than a clean one?

When you're dusting for fingerprints!

Why couldn't the license drive?
No one would permit it.

What was so amazing about the tire?
It spoke.

Why did the dumbbell go through the traffic light?
It didn't want to weight.

What happened when the car hit the food processor?
They had a little fender blender.

What did the bridge say to the car?
Are you coming over?

How was the demolition derby?

A smash!

Why did the spices drive so slow?
They had plenty of thyme.

How did the screwdriver get lost?
It got turned around.

How do circles travel on vacation?
Round-trip.

What happened to the calculator's new car?
It was totaled.

How long does it take to lose a race?
Only a 2nd.

Why are geese rude drivers?

Because they're always honking!

How did the hay get out of jail?
It paid its bale.

What did the booth say to the money?
I tolled you so!

Why was the corn so rich?
It had a lot of stocks.

How did the number know the decimal forgot her?
He couldn't place her for a moment.

How can you find out what a wall weighs?
You scale it.

What did the four quarters say about buying something?
Let's go fifty-fifty.

What did the number zero say about its problem?
Nothing.

What did the phone say about the math problem?
I think I have the wrong number.

What does it sound like when a number and a rope argue?
Was two, was knot! WAS TWO!

How do the even numbers divide things up?
Equally.

What happened when the owl put on the brakes?

The car came to a screeching halt!

Why did the racecar get rid of its driver?

It kept driving him up a wall!

Why was the first number in the room so lonely?
She was the only one.

Why did the motorcycle keep falling asleep?
It was two tired.

What kind of car do chickens drive?

A coupe!

What do car mechanics do when they get tired?
They take a brake.

Where do cars like to cook?
On their grilles.

What kind of car comes with its own makeup?
A compact.

What do farmers like to race?
Stalk cars.

What does a bowler put in its trunk?
A spare.

How did the rhino tell
the hippo to get out of its way?

It used its horn!

What did the basketball team drive to the game?
A squad car.

How do most dogs get around?
In a waggin'.

Where do cars keep cool?
In car pools.

How do you keep from upsetting a tire?
You tread lightly.

Why was the car so happy?
It was on a joyride.

Why did the road have to take anger management?
Because of its rage.

When do roads get the maddest?
When you cross the line.

Where do shovels ride in a car?
In the bucket seats.

What kind of cars do eggs drive?
Hatchbacks.

How do cars hang on to their money?
They clutch it.

THE JOKIEST JOKING JOKE BOOK EVER WRITTEN . . . NO JOKE!

What happened when the car told a joke?

It didn't get much mileage out of it.

Why didn't the mechanic tell the car about her dent?

He didn't want to o-fender.

Why did the car have to drink slower?

It was a guzzler.

What do lightning bolts like to drive?

Hot rods.

Why did the car stop for the picnic?

It was in park.

How come the elevator wasn't working?

Because it was floored!

Why didn't the chicken get hit when it crossed the road?
It was very clucky.

How are engines like cats?
Sometime they roar and sometimes they purr.

Why can't lips drive?
They smack right into things.

How do golf carts get where they are going?
They putter around.

How was the car after the accident?
It was a wreck.

Why did the water go out for cross-country?
It liked running.

10
I'VE GOT YOUR NUMBER—
Number Riddles & Jokes, etc.

Where do all the numbers eat dinner?

At the times table!

Why was the calendar so hard to read?

Its days were all mixed up.

Why was the calendar moving so slowly?

It was feeling week.

What did one hand say to the other when their days were numbered?

I'm counting on you!

Why does the number twelve
always seem so sleepy?

Because it's a doze-n!

Why couldn't the car door figure out how to open?

It couldn't get a handle on it.

Why were the numbers such a problem?

They were always up two something.

Why weren't the numbers friends with the magnet?

They were too negative.

What did the numbers do with everything at the times tables?

They eight it up.

Why was the man's watch on backwards?

It did an about-face.

Why were the math problems
in such good shape?

They did their exercises!

What do baby math problems drink?
Formulas.

Why did the scientist get rid of his clock?
It was a matter of time.

What did the father number call his boy?
My sum.

What did the money say about its change?
It was worth it.

How did the fishermen know there was a mistake on their bill?
They caught it.

How do you get a penny in the mail?
You get one cent.

Why did the money stop by the bank?
It was paying them a visit.

How do pillars talk to their families?
They column.

What do birds retire on?
Their nest eggs.

What do your dishes like to do on Friday nights?
Bowl.

What is something only two equations can have?

A problem child!

Why was the cow mad at the dart?
For hitting the bull's eye!

What do you call it when two numbers have a baby?
A new addition.

Why was the number so proud?
Because everyone counted on him.

Why was math such a problem?
Nothing added up.

Why couldn't the calculator share its lunch?
Because everybody wanted sum.

What was the math problem's favorite dessert?

The pie chart!

Why can't you tell when a ruler is kidding?

It keeps a straight face!

Why did the mathematician need a ladder?

Things were starting to add up.

How did the gymnasts feel about changing places with the dancers?

They were pretty flexible!

What do cowboys do with partial numbers?
They round them up.

What do rabbits like to add?
Hole numbers.

Why was the compass so frustrated?
It couldn't get the right angle.

What do confused problems ask?
What's the difference?

What do big numbers wear?
Plus-sizes.

How did the students feel about the abacus?

They counted on him.

Why do bunnies do so well in math?

They are very good at multiplying.

Are all numbers the same?

More or less.

Where does the inchworm like to play?

In a yard.

Why didn't the witch like Dorothy?

She was a goody two-shoes.

Why was the clock always bored?

It had too much time on its hands!

Did the adding machine like the paper?

Totally!

What did the watch do at the end of the day?

It clocked out.

Why didn't the phone win the lottery?

It got the wrong number.

How do numbers get in a line?

They count off.

What do a sock and a shoe have in common?

They are both about a foot long.

What do you get when you mix a clock, a tree, and a tornado?

Someone who knows when it's time to pull up their roots and leaf.

Why did the numbers step out of line?
Because they were out of order.

Why didn't the house like its number?
It was odd.

What number will never lose a race?
Number one.

What kind of art do math teachers like most?
Paint by number.

What instrument can a sheep and the number two make?
A two baa.

Why was the year so spicy?
It had four seasons.

What do you get when you cross a frog with a calendar?
A leap year.

What do you do if you want to be a minute older?
You wait a minute.

What did the thumb give the fingers for typing so well?
A thumbs up!

What do you call a day with 25 hours?
The next day!

Why did the clock spray itself with bug spray?

It had a tick!

What time do wristwatches like to have dinner?
Ate o'clock.

Why was the hour hand in time-out?
It struck twelve.

When can 12 turn into 1?
When it's a foot.

Why did 2 and 4 kick out number 3?
To get even.

How many people are coming to the ice-skating party?
Figure 8.

Which one of the fonts was the bravest?

The bold one!

Which part of the clock will never come first?
The second hand.

How did the cowboy get so wet?
His 10-gallon hat had a leak.

Why can't two-headed aliens be trusted?
They're two-faced.

Why did the rocket struggle in math?
It kept counting backwards.

What did the thirsty clock do?
Drank from an hourglass.

What did the weatherman get when he
broke both arms and both legs?

Four-casts!

What do you get when you have two apples?
A pear.

Why couldn't the measuring tape move?
Its foot was asleep.

What kind of dancing do numbers like to do?
The two-step.

What is the fraction's favorite part of the football game?
The last half.

What did the line figure say when its pet bird came up missing?
Polygon.

What do numbers use to count?

Their digits!

How can a super number make itself bigger?
It can use its powers.

What shapes do big rigs like to draw?
Semicircles.

What did the number zero say about giving up its place?
Nada chance.

How did the numbers feel about being separated?
They were a little divided over it.

What did the numbers say as they got ready to leave together?
We are all set.

Why were the pennies always laughing?

They had a cents of humor!

What did the guitar use to count?
Bass numbers.

What numbers are the best to play ball with?
Round ones.

What angles are never wrong?
Right angles.

What measuring device makes the best leader?
A ruler.

What numbers are the deepest?
Root numbers.

Why was the calculator so quiet?

It had nothing to add!

Which numbers are not the most optimistic?
Negative numbers.

How does Rhom get around?
On a Rhombus.

How do cameras practice their numbers?

With flash cards!

What do you call making cake,
after cake, after cake, after cake?

Duplicaking it!

What happened when 19 and 20 had a race?
Twenty one.

Why weren't three and four shutting the door?
They didn't one, two.

Why did the number one think it was so special?
It was the only 1 in a million.

What did the twelve cookies say when the thirteenth one hopped in?
Dozen matter.

Why are thermometers so smart?
They have lots of degrees.

Did the godmother use her wand in time?

Yes, she was fairy fast!

Why did Pinocchio ask so many questions?
He was very nosey.

What do you call a poem you can say over and over again?
A reverse.

What do you get when you combine a rock with a newspaper?
Hard times.

What did Humpty Dumpty do after the fall?
He went to pieces.

What happened after Jack broke his crown?
It all sort of went downhill from there.

Why did Thomas get in trouble at the table?
For chugging down his drink.

What do all of the storybook characters think of Red Riding Hood?
She's cape-able.

What did the Three Little Pigs say when there was no one at the door?
Werewolf?

How long did it take to get rid of the dragon?

Two Knights!

Why couldn't Cinderella play baseball?

She was always running away from the ball!

How do clocks start their bedtime stories?
Once upon a time . . .

When did the king ask for the royal joker?
Jest in time.

Which storybook character could be an author?
Little Red Writing Hood.

What did one story say to the other?
You're telling me!

What do you have when you have two ducks and a goose?
A game!

Who did little Miss Peep invite to the dance?

Her Bo!

What did Miss Muffet say when
the spider asked for her curds?

No Whey!

What did the mirror say to the Queen when Snow White won?

You need to face it.

What did Jack say the second time he went down the hill?

I'm not falling for that again!

How come Jack can never be king?

Because he broke his crown.

Where do you keep a wild squash?

In a zoochini.

How did Alice finally figure out where she was?

She put on her looking glasses.

Why can't the three bears ever open the door?

Goldie locks it!

Why was Baa Baa always getting into trouble?

Because he was the black sheep of the family.

How do you find a book in a hospital?

You page it.

What's the last thing an author will ever write?

The end.

Why wouldn't the artist read the cartoon novel?

It was too graphic.

Why was the story so mad at the writer?

He was plotting against it.

Why did the book go to the chiropractor?

To have its spine adjusted!

What were Baby Buntings first and last words?
Bye-Bye.

Why was the whole Miss Muffet thing such a drama?
It was an itsy bitsy spider.

Where did Peter Peter's wife go?
The pumpkin eater.

How did the pirate know it was time for tea?
Polly Put the Kettle On.

Why was Wee Willie winking?
He had something in his eye.

Why were the flowers so smart?
The roses are read to.

Why was Simon so mad?
Someone called him simple.

When do kings worry the most?
When the reign stops.

How did the book feel about its beginnings?
Fairly contents.

How can you tell when a nursery rhyme is ready for bed?
It's Wynken, Blynken, and Nodding.

Why didn't Hansel and Gretel follow the trail?

It was too crumby!

What did the pans say when the vegetable's story grew longer?
Asparagus the details and go on.

Why wouldn't the porridge go outside in the summer?
It was too hot.

What did the spider say when Miss Muffet finished all of her curds?
Whey to go!

How did the pie get Little Jack to talk about what the thumb had done to it?
It cornered him.

How much garbage did the black sheep have?
Three bags full.

How did the book talk to its friends?
By text.

Why was the library book so detached?
It checked out.

Why was the book first in the race?
It was bound to win.

Why were the words and spaces agreeing?
They were on the same page.

What happened when the giraffe wrote a book?
It's a long story.

What did Juliet say when she climbed into the boat?

Row-me-o!

Why couldn't the story stay at the hotel?
It was all booked up.

What did the frog say to the tadpole?
I froget what were we doing?

Where did the story go?
It booked it out of here.

What did Little Bo have to say about the lost sheep?
Not a peep.

How did the fairy tale end?
It was kind of Grimm.

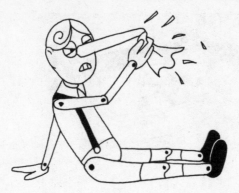

What does Pinocchio get when he blows his nose?

Splinters!

What did Little Boy Blew?
His nose.

What did the gardener say that made everyone think he was color blind?
Lavender's blue.

What nursery rhyme is never told in the desert?
Rain Rain Go Away

What did Prince Charming and Cinderella do at the dance?
They had a ball.

What sound did Peter Piper make when he was little?
A Pitter patter.

How do chickens have such nice eyebrows?
They pluck them.

How is Cinderella always prepared for sports?
She's wearing a ball gown.

How did everyone learn that Wilbur was some pig?
On Charlotte's Web site.

What is most attracted to Iron Man?
Magnets.

Where do the magicians play when they're kids?
In magic tree houses.

How did the Hatter find the whole Alice dilemma?

Maddening!

Why wouldn't Rapunzel come out of her room?

She was having a bad hair day!

Where do spies get their flowers?
In a secret garden.

How much cheese does the Wimpy Kid like on his sandwich?
Just a touch.

What do ghosts hate to drive through?
Phantom tollbooths.

What did one yellow creature say to the other yellow creature after he did him a favor?
Thanks a minion.

What do silly birds write in?
Stork Diaries.

How do you know when a wolf
doesn't have a winning hand in cards?

He huffs when he bluffs!

Which snicket is the most sour?
Lemony Snicket.

Where does the street start?
Where the sidewalk ends.

What did the stools say when they got on the bus?
Don't Let the Pigeon Drive.

What do you call it when you play sports on an empty stomach?
Hunger Games.

Who stole everyone's thunder?
The lightning thief.

What kind of net was stuck
to the knight in shining armor?

A magnet!

What did the spider say to her new friend?
Hi, Fly Guy.

Which superhero is a lousy boxer?
Captain Underpants.

How did everyone know the book was happy?
It had a big Smile.

How did Rapunzel and her hair feel about each other?
They never wanted to be a part.

What bear is the biggest complainer?
Whiny The Pooh

Which storybook character could be an author?

Little Red Writing Hood!

What was the scared baby goat's favorite book?
Diary of a Wimpy Kid.

How did Spider Man meet Spider Woman?
On the Web.

Who was the biggest king in history?
King Kong.

How did Captain Underpants get so strong?
He used to be a boxer.

12
RIDDLED WITH FUN—
Famous Characters, etc.

How do cars eat?

Off their license plates!

Why did Mr. Potato Head look so sad?
Because his mouth was on upside down.

Why did the circus performer get so tired at work?
He was juggling two jobs.

What kind of haircuts do sponges get?
Bobs.

Why did the snake get lost?

It was rattled!

What do you get when you combine a pirate and a bird?
A Jack Sparrow.

What do you get when you cross Bozo with a goldfish?
A clown fish.

How does Count Dracula play baseball?
With a vampire bat.

Why was Mr. Potato Head so embarrassed?
He picked someone else's nose.

What is Shaggy's favorite hobby?
Scooby diving.

THE JOKIEST JOKING JOKE BOOK EVER WRITTEN . . . NO JOKE!

What do you call Princess Sofia's problems?

A royal mess!

If a mountain and a valley had a baby, what would they name it?
Cliff.

What is Anna and Elsa's favorite game?
Freeze tag.

What happens when Sponge Bob pretends to be a pirate?
He walks the plankton.

Which bunny can drive you crazy?
Bugs.

What did Puss do when someone complimented his shoes?
He gave them the boot.

Why was the tree so loud?

It had a lot of bark!

How did Donatello the Ninja Turtle finally get a girlfriend?
He finally came out of his shell.

How did the Seven Dwarfs feel about being short?
They under-stood completely.

What was the first thing Thomas did with his dog when he brought it home?
He trained it.

Why did the king believe the knight's story?
He sword it was true.

What did the skunk say to the only pink cat it had ever seen?
Hello, kitty.

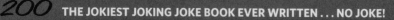

How can you tell if a cartoon is happy?
It's very animated.

Where do chicken jokes come from?
The funny farm.

What one word can change everything?
Abracadabra.

What do you call a clown who wears his nose on his ear?
A Bozo.

Why are pickles so slow?
They tend to dill-y-dally.

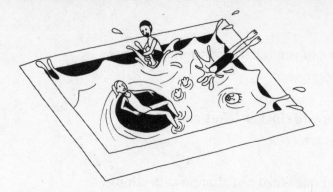

How did the kids like the swimming pool?

It made a big splash!

Where do pigs go to get clean?
The hogwash.

Why was the bowling ball wet?

There was rain in the gutters

How do bees communicate?

They use buzz words!

Where did Loopsy go on her trip?
To La La Land.

How do canyons eat?
They gorge themselves.

Why was the door so nervous?
It was unhinged.

How did the pig get out of the mud?
It was snort of a problem.

When is your hair noisy?
When it has bangs.

Why did the water have to calm down?
It spouted off.

How many friends did the bell bring to the party?
It brought the whole clang.

What do baby brooks do?
Babble.

Why was the toilet red?
It was flushed.

How does a runner drink milk?
She laps it up.

What does Barbie think about while she is sleeping?

Her dream home!

How does a tongue draw attention to itself?

When it sticks out!

What do trains hang on to when they go downstairs?
The rails.

How do you know when a bell has something to say?
It chimes in.

Why did the percussionists have to take a break?
They were drumming up some trouble.

What happened to the mad scientist's plan?
It fizzled out.

What do tunes say when they're stumped?
Hum.

Which cartoon character spends
the most time on Twitter?

Tweety Bird!

Why was the nail in bed?
It had a pounding headache.

What did the pot do with the chili's secret?
It spilled the beans.

How did the chicken do at impersonating a duck?
Just clucky.

How did the road feel about twin chickens crossing it?
Sort of double-crossed.

Why wouldn't the cube go to the show?
It was a blockbuster.

What did the doorknob say to the door?
It's my turn.

Why did the potato chip stop the car?
There was a dip in the road.

What do plastic bags wear on formal occasions?
Zip ties.

What room did the racket stay in?
10 S.

What sport was the bank good at?
Vaulting.

What did the butter say to Mr. Potato Head?

You make me melt!

What would the tree do if it had a window?

Add a little shade!

What do you call a silly pickle?
A daffy dill.

Why couldn't the boxing gloves get along?
They weren't a good match.

Why did the pickles climb into the truck?
The door was ajar.

Why are pianos good with locks?
They have a lot of keys.

Where do toilet paper rolls sleep?
Under the sheets.

What did Anna do when she forgot
her part in the show?

She froze!

What did the juicer do to the lemons?
Gave them some ade.

Where does
Princess Celestia go
when she gets sick?

The horspital!

Why do flowers work out?

They don't want to be pansies.

Why was the fir tree so sad?

He pined for the other tree the moment he cedar.

What did the pumpkins think of the other crop?

It was a little corny.

Why was the necklace so bored?

It was tired of hanging around.

What's the best way to listen to fireworks?

With a boom box.

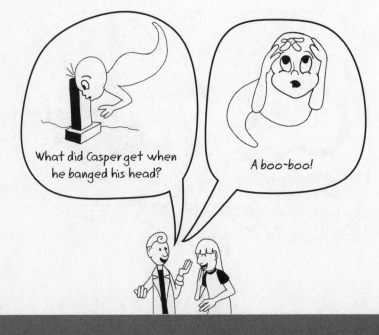

What happened when the laundry started wrestling?
The clothes were pinned.

What does a hero eat his soup out of?
A super bowl.

What did the lamp post on its page?
Something enlightening.

Where do snowmen go to dance?
Snow balls.

Why did the shrub quit working?
It was bushed.

What were the two garden hoses expecting?

A little squirt!

Why did the candle get sent to its room?

It had a meltdown!

Why was the coffee so upset?
Someone mugged it.

Why was the tennis ball shocked?
Someone took it to court.

What happened when the quilt told the needle a joke?
He had her in stitches.

Did the drill finally finish its supper?
Every last bit.

Why did the officer stop the yarn?
It was weaving in and out of traffic.

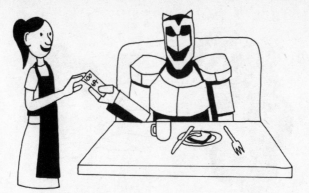

What did the Transformer tell
the waitress as it was leaving?

Keep the change!

How do you know when your dishes are in trouble?
They're in hot water.

What was Rumpelstiltskin doing in the Olympics?
Going for the gold.

How come the Tin Man never needed a bath?
He was always squeaky clean.

What do you call a tiny onion?
A Minion.

How did Sponge Bob like being in the pool?
He soaked it up.

How did Oh save the Boovs?
He had a good Tip.

How do trees sleep?

Like logs!

What do you get when you cross a beetle and a rabbit?
Bugs Bunny.

How come Jacques made Nemo go through "The Ring of Fire"?
Because he was shellfish.

What did the ogre do about all of his problems?
Shrekked them off.

What do you get when you cross a black sheep with a baby cat?
A Baaad Kitty.

How did Mator's friend get around?
Like lightning.

13
THE TROUBLE WITH JOKES—
Jokes About Getting in Trouble, etc.

Why couldn't the alligator talk?

It had a frog in its throat!

Why was Yes always in trouble?
It didn't "no."

How does your laundry solve its problems?
It just sorts them out.

Why was the punctuation put in time-out?
It wouldn't comma down.

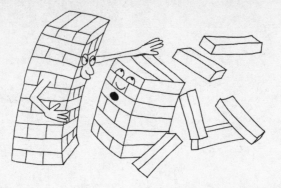

Why was one game of Jenga mad at the other?

It knocked its blocks off!

Why did the drill have to go in a different drawer of the toolbox?
It bit someone.

What did the captain do when his ship ran into trouble?
He re-PORT-ed it.

What did the earthquake say when it was blamed for all the mess?
It wasn't my fault.

What do you do when a clock is bad?
You give it a time-out.

What did one screw tell the other when they ran into a problem?
Use your head.

Why was the witch moving a stick around in her cauldron?
She was trying to stir up trouble.

Why was the little brain sent to its room?
To think about what it did.

Why did Merry go round?
The other rides were in the way.

What kind of cleanser do dogs hate the most?
Spot remover.

Why was Santa having such a problem at the workshop?
He couldn't control his elf.

Why was everyone laughing at the pet shop?

Someone asked "what did that dog doo?"

What do you call a dog that isn't potty trained?

Puddles!

What did the piggy bank say when it was mad?
Save it!

How did Nemo learn his lesson?
He had a little schooling.

What caused the commotion in the washing machine?
One of the pieces of clothing socked the other!

How did the submarine answer the question?
I sink so.

Why did the toilet get into trouble?
It ran in the bathroom.

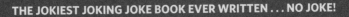

THE JOKIEST JOKING JOKE BOOK EVER WRITTEN . . . NO JOKE!

How do you know when a notebook is in trouble?
It's in a bind.

Did you read the book about the hammer?
It was a nail-biter.

Why did the piece of paper get mad at the pen?
It was out of line.

What do you call it if you are in trouble more than once?
Two much trouble.

Who takes care of the problems in the bathroom?
The toilet handles them.

How do you get a shoe to stop talking?

You put a sock in it!

Why was the pan struggling with her problem?
She didn't know how to handle it.

Why did the pen get into so much trouble?
It was dotting the T's and making the I's cross.

Did you hear about the gum and the dryer?
It was kind of a sticky situation.

Why couldn't the lolli ever be a balloon?
Because the lolli popped.

How did the glasses know the clock was late?
They were watching him.

What did the dartboard say to the bad dart player?

What's the point?!

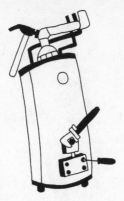

What did the tools do when they had a problem?

They fixed it!

What did the balloon say right before the party?
I hope this isn't a blowout.

What do you get when you mix a sprained elbow with a syringe?
A slingshot.

Why couldn't the cube remember anything?
Because she blocked it out.

Why weren't the leaves talking?
They had a fallout.

What did the hunter say about the rabbit sitting by his trap?
Its not gonna hoppin'.

What did the ballerina do when she had a problem?

Tip-toed around it!

Why couldn't the magician put his arm in his shirt?
He had something up his sleeve.

Why did the fish go to the doctor?

It was feeling eel!

222 THE JOKIEST JOKING JOKE BOOK EVER WRITTEN . . . NO JOKE!

What do you call it when a bunch of fish steal your boat?
Something fishy rowing on.

How did the microscope solve its problem?
It didn't, it made it bigger.

Why did the needle have trouble understanding?
It just couldn't get the point.

What did the needle say when it got in trouble?
Darn it.

When did the wire realize it was in trouble?
When it got grounded.

Why did the rug get into trouble?

For just laying around!

What do childish skunks do when they are upset?

They make a big stink about it!

How did the pen and paper get into trouble?

They didn't know write from wrong.

Why was March never clean?

Because April got all the showers!

What is a baby bird's favorite game?
Beak-a-boo!

Why were the riddle and the pun worried about the joke?
It was sort of sick.

What did the mice say when the cheese was all gone?
Rats!

How do you know when your mascara is upset?
It lashes out at you.

What's the basketball's favorite place for donuts?
Dunkin'.

Why was the laundry complaining about flapping in the wind?
It was left hung out to dry.

What did the breaker box do when someone switched its switches?
It blew a fuse.

Why was the cushion moving so carefully?
It was on pins and needles.

Why was the fox in so much trouble with the mama bird?
It was walking on eggshells.

How did the barbed wire feel about its job?
It was on the fence about it.

Why was the rabbit wearing a hat?

It was having a bad hare day!

What do pigs like to write with?

Pigpens!

What did the camel tell the soda pop?
That's the last straw.

Why was the stomach a little uneasy?
It had a gut feeling something was wrong.

How did the magician make all of his problems go away?
With a little hocus pocus.

How do you know you have a problem with your stairs?
When it escalates.

What do grumpy mountains have?
Bad altitudes.

What did the tub do to stop feeling so full?
It pulled the plug.

What happens when you leave an apple in the sun too long?
You get an apple crisp.

How did the needle feel about being in trouble?
It didn't give a darn.

What happens if a bird flaps its wings a lot?
It sores.

Why did the basketball think it was in trouble?
Someone put it in a cage.

Why are guitars always upset?
Because they fret about things.

What do you call a sweater's problem?
A real snag.

How did the pushpins tell the bulletin board there was a problem?
Very tackfully.

How did the people know the mannequin wasn't real?
He was a poser.

How did the muffins become brownies?
There was a mix-up.

What did the envelopes do about getting stamped on?

They had to address it!

What did the cat say when it got hurt?

Me ouch!

How did the shoe get into trouble?

It stepped right into a mess.

What kind of fish is always prepared for a fight?

A swordfish!

Why did the phones have such a problem when they had a baby?
They didn't know what to call it.

What did the trash can say to the two fighting bags?
Take it outside.

What did the stomach think about its newest problem?
It was trying to digest it.

How did the carrot know the onion was hurt?

He was crying!

Why can you never tell lettuce that she's pretty?
Because it always goes to her head.

What does a really bad cold put on its pancakes?
Cough syrup.

Why did the blender chop up the cubes?
It just wanted to break the ice.

What do your arms and cherries have in common?
They both have pits.

What time do cookies hate the most of all?
Crunch time.

Where does really, really dry cake live?
The dessert.

Why was the hen too tired to lay more eggs?
Because she was cooped.

Why was the dough off by itself?
It kneaded to be alone.

Why did the butter always lose?
Because it was creamed.

Why did the lettuce take the bus?
Because it had to leaf.

What did the one straw say to the other straw when times got tough?
Suck it up.

Why didn't the bread rise?
There was no knead.

What do you get when you mix sheet music with syrup?
Sticky notes.

How did the banana get away fast?

It peeled out of the kitchen!

What made the pickles' lives so bumpy?

They were a little jarred!

How quickly did the pudding and milk become friends?
Almost instantly.

What kind of water never runs downstream?
Bottled water.

Where do ice like to get together to work?
In a cube-ical.

What's the funniest thing about an egg?
Its yolk.

Why were the melons laughing?
They were having a ball.

What happens when you tell an egg a joke?

It cracks up!

How do you see a cabbage in the dark?
Head lights.

How do you get information from a hamburger?
You grill it.

What did one pretzel say to the other?

Why are you so twisted?

Why did the cake go shopping all the time?

Its frosting was really rich!

Why are people so sleepy after they eat?
They're at a rest-aurant.

What kind of water doesn't pour?
Ice.

Why was the fruit salad mad at the grapes?
They were raisin trouble.

Why was the potato creepy?
It kept an eye on everyone.

Who do the chocolate bunnies hang out with at Easter?
Their peeps.

What did the bread say when it was put in the oven?
I'm toast!

Why was the plum so upset?
It got pruned.

What did the spaghetti say to the macaroni?
You look a little bent out of shape.

What happened to the cabbage?
It laughed its head off.

What did the corn call their leader?
Kernel.

Where does lettuce go to get changed?

In the dressing room!

Why did the milk want to join the circus?

It liked jug -gling!

How did the peach know it needed glasses?
Things were getting a little fuzzy.

Why did the peach tell the other fruits to stop the car?
She had to make a pit stop.

Why did the raspberry get in trouble?
For being berry mean.

What do you get when you put your green beans on ice?
Cool beans!

Why did all the vegetables in the fridge think the celery was a little weird?
It kept stalking them.

Which beans are the coldest?

Chili beans!

What does really old sugar need?
A cane.

Why couldn't the beef stick draw a straight line?
It was a little jerky.

What vegetable can be really flat when it wants to be?
Squash.

How do vegetables ask nicely?
They say "peas, may I."

How did the doughnut get caught telling a lie?
It had a hole in its story.

What did one package of meat call the other?
Turkey!

When do vegetables like music the best?

When you turnip the volume!

What kind of cookie can
laugh and draw at the same time?

A snicker doodle!

What did the tortillas do with the missing dessert?
No one knows, they kept it under wraps.

How can you tell when the dairy items are scared?
The cheese gets strung out and the milk shakes.

Where does a piece of meat hate to be tickled?
In the ribs!

What did the salt call the sugar?
Sweetie!

Which vegetable is the skinniest?
The string beans.

Why did the olive never eat?
It was stuffed.

How did the meats keep track of the utensils?

They steaked them out.

What do gold bars eat for lunch?

Chicken nuggets.

How did the macaroni get out of the hot water it was in?

It used its noodle.

Why did the soup just keep getting hotter and hotter?

It was stewing about something.

What do you call a bad citrus fruit?

A real lemon.

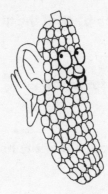

Why can corn hear so well?

When they're all ears!

Why did everyone leave the cereal alone?
It was a little flakey.

How do you get a fish to answer a question?
You grill it.

Why wouldn't the mollusk talk?
No one knows, it just clammed up.

What did the sausage say to the pancake?
Do you smell something bacon?

How did the carrot feel about the new shredder?
It's grate!

What do potatoes call their kids?

Tater tots!

What main dish is the laziest of all?
Meatloaf.

Why wouldn't the egg go back to the beach?
It was already fried.

What is the worst thing you can call a crustacean?
A shrimp.

Why were the rolls yelling?
They kneaded help.

What citrus drink is everyone's favorite?
Orange, are juice surprised?

What do cherries have when they are sad?

Pitty parties!

What did the lettuce say about the tomatoes?
They don't seem to carrot all.

What did the freezer say to the hot-tempered popsicles?
Chill.

How do you make fake bread?
Out of play dough.

Why did the grapes come in from the sun?
No raisin.

Why did the pretzels get mad at the chips and sour cream?
They were kind of dippy.

Why are turkeys good musicians?

They all have drumsticks!

What did the pancake do when it saw the griddle?
It flipped out.

Why did the milk want to join the circus?
It liked jug-gling.

What did one ear of corn say when it dropped the other?
Shucks!

Why were the eggs so exhausted?
They had to scramble to get everything done.

Why did the broccoli leave the catering business?
He wanted to quit while he was still a head.

What do most vegetables wear to the pool?

Their zucchinis!

What food is the hardest to clean out of a pan?
Fish sticks.

What did the toaster tell the bread?
Crust me, I know butter.

Whose hot dog is that?
Frank's.

Why did the boy laugh at his hot dog?
Because it was bun-ny.

Why did the pickle get kicked out of class?
For being dilly.

What did the two pieces of bread say to the peanut butter?
You're not going to come between us.

What does the ice cream like to ride?
A popsicle.

What would a banana be without a b?
A nana.

What do you get when you cross a chicken and a bush?
An eggplant.

Why did the apple want to date the clementine?
She was a real cutie.

What did the lemon do when it got into a real pinch?

It had to squeeze by!

15
ZOOLARIOUS—Jokes About Animals

What do you get when you combine a monkey, a scholar, and some bananas?

A bunch of bananas that know better than to monkey around.

What do you get when you cross a dog with a bull?

A best friend who can always give you a buck.

What did the baby duck do when its parents went to see the doctor?
It stayed in the wading room.

Where do horses live?
In their neigh-borhood.

How do frogs die?
They croak.

What did the horse say when the cow tried to take its food?
Hay!

What do you get when you cross a pig's tail with a potato?
Curly fries.

What happens when you mix a pig with a fishing rod?
It becomes a reel ham.

What do you get when you put a Chihuahua in a pile of leaves?
Dog gone if I know.

What do you get when you give a chimpanzee a TV?
A swing set.

What do elephants always take to the pool?
Their trunks.

What do you get when you mix a lamb with a yellow jacket?
A really sharp wool coat.

What do you get when you cross a coyote and a primate?

A howler monkey!

What kind of fish is the best hugger?

A cuttlefish!

What do you call a cross between a kangaroo and a legume?
A jumping bean.

What do you get when you cross a fly with Bigfoot?
A fly that can swat you.

What do cows use when they drive?
Bull horns.

What kind of underwear do dogs wear?
Boxers.

How do you hide a camel?
You use camelflage.

What kind of shark is the handiest?

A hammerhead!

What do Santa's deer wear when it's really wet outside?
Reincoats.

Why was the kangaroo in a bad mood?
It was feeling a little pouchy.

What do ducks do when you tell them a joke?

They quack up!

254   THE JOKIEST JOKING JOKE BOOK EVER WRITTEN . . . NO JOKE!

What did the fish have to wear to class everyday?
A school uniform.

What kind of sweaters do tortoises wear?
Turtlenecks.

What do you get when you cross a Chihuahua and a skunk?
A dog that's a little stinky.

What do you get when you mix a poodle and a porcupine?
A dog that's a little prickly about its haircut.

What do you get when you mix an eel with a quilt?
An electric blanket.

How does the kangaroo know what time it is?

It uses its pocket watch!

What do you get when you cross a cobra and a plant?
Poison ivy.

Why couldn't the zebra sing?
Because it was hoarse.

What did everyone love the gerbil?
Because it was mice.

How did the eagle know that the owl thought she was pretty?
His head spun around.

What do you call a giraffe's underpants?
Long underwear.

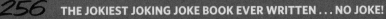

Why were the rams inseparable?

They locked horns!

What do you call an unfunny egg?
No yolk.

What kind of shoes do sloths wear?
Loafers.

What do dogs wear at the hospital?
Lab coats.

What do kangaroos wear to weddings?
Jump suits.

How do snakes keep their socks up?
With garters.

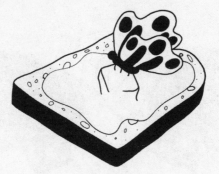

What do you get when a bug lands on your toast?

A butterfly!

What do fish wear when they get out of the water?
Flip-flops.

What did the kangaroo say to the rabbit?
Pardon me, I'm feeling a little jumpy.

What kind of dog do you use to keep warm?
An Afghan hound.

What kind of dogs are the hungriest?
Chow Chows

What do you get when you cross a lamp with a night crawler?
A glowworm.

How did the scallop get the jar open?

It used its mussels!

What kind of shark can heal you after it bites?
A nurse shark.

How did the walrus plug up the hole in his house?
With a seal.

What kind of fish can you carry in your pocket?
A silver dollar.

What do you say to an unfunny hare?
That's not bunny!

What do you get when you put antlers on a cow?
A mooooooooose.

What do you call a crazy squirrel?

A nutcase!

What do you get when you cross a chimpanzee and a piece of fruit?

A grape.

What do you call a tattletale mouse?

A rat.

What do you call a pig on a bush?

A hedge hog.

What do you get when you combine a toad with a pig?

A warthog.

How come no one believed the rodent?

He was squirrely.

What did the cat think of all of the attention?

It was purrfect!

What do you get when you cross a bunny and a lawnmower?

A grasshopper.

Why was the ox laughing at the farmer?

Because the yoke was on him!

What do you call an angry bear?

Furrious!

What do you call a dog that can fly?
A beagle.

What do you call an insect you're related to?
An ant.

How do fish eat cereal?
From a fish bowl.

Did the fisherman really buy the fishy story?
Hook, line, and sinker.

Which bird is the biggest coward?
A chicken.

What do you get when you
cross a singer and a gorilla?

A gorillalalalalalala!

What do you get when you cross a lamb and a monkey?

A baa boon.

How come nobody wanted to hang out with the crustacean?

He was crabby.

Which bird does the best at scouting?

An eagle.

What did one salamander tell the other when he got the answer right?

I newt.

How come the panther didn't believe the tiger?

Because he was lion.

How do you know when a fish is happy?

It's kind of bubbly!

What do you get when you cross a lane with a track star?
A roadrunner.

How does a fish find out what it weighs?
It uses its scales.

What did the clams think of the oysters?
They were a little shellfish.

What do you get when you cross a rooster and a beetle?
A cockroach.

What candy do sharks dislike the most?
Jawbreakers.

How do jockeys ride across the ocean?

By seahorse!

What did the calves say when their mother told them to go to bed?
Do we hoof to?

Why did the lobster turn red?
He was steamed.

Which marsupial is the best actor?
An opossum; it's always playing dead.

Which bird takes the most chances?
An ostrich; it's always sticking its neck out.

Why wouldn't the leopard move out of its seat?
He didn't want to change his spot.

What did the birds do when they heard there was a sale?
They flocked to it.

Where do little dogs stay when they go camping?
In pup tents.

What do dogs usually do when there is a problem?
They flea from it.

Why were the worms nervous?
Someone was robin their hole.

What do you call a piece of bacon with thorns?
A pork-upine.

How come the ferret had no friends?

Because he was a weasel!

What do you get when you cross a gecko and a sausage?
A salaminder.

What's the cleanest fish in the ocean?
A sponge.

What do you call an angry reptile?
A snapping turtle.

What do you call a bear that's happy and sad at the same time?
A polar bear.

Which rodent is the best at fetching things?
A gofer.

How did one porcupine make the other porcupine laugh?

It was acting quilly!

Why couldn't the joke get around very well?

It was lame.

What can appear, disappear, and reappear whenever it wants?

The word "appear."

When the land and the water were arguing, which side did the shell take?
The sea's side.

Why did one woodpecker think the other was sick?
He looked a little peckish.

Why did the volcano never erupt?
Because it was a lava not a hater.

Why was the lightning so bad at bowling?
Lightning never strikes twice.

Why did the chicken have to go to time-out?
Because of its fowl language.

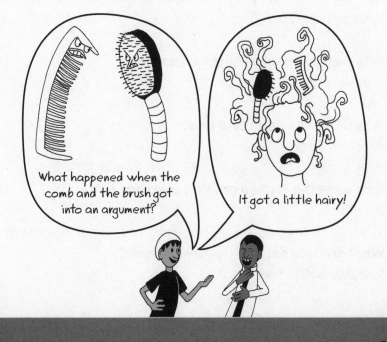

What happened when the comb and the brush got into an argument?

It got a little hairy!

What kind of card does a frog
use when it goes shopping?

Debbit!

How did the puzzle get itself together?
It just sort of fell into place.

Why were the shoes going backwards?
They were retracing their steps.

Why didn't the drum ever lose?
It couldn't be beat.

How come the camera couldn't concentrate?
It lost focus.

What decision did the tree have to make?
Take it or leaf it.

What part of a candy bar likes music the most?

The wrapper!

What do you call a really mean cow?
A Bully.

Where do most lions live?
On Mane Street.

Why was the balloon getting so tired?
It had been up all night.

How did the swimmer win the lottery?
She had a stroke of luck.

How do the nuts get anything accomplished?
They get cracking.

Why did the cough drop quit?
It couldn't hack it anymore.

Why couldn't the margarine do its job?
It wouldn't stick to it.

Why did the fingernail lose the race?
It wasn't that quick.

Why did the doctor have to check the treasure?
It was having chest pains.

What do you call a fake deer?
A play doe.

What do you get when you
put a clock in the trash?

A waste of time!

How did they know the chimney was sick?

It had a flue.

What kind of animal can you put in your hair?

Moose!

Why did one flower get mad at the other flower?
It wouldn't leaf.

When can you get lost in the corn?
When it's a maize.

Which academy did the orange attend?
The navel academy.

How do dogs take a break from their movies?
They paws them.

What did the jet think of its trip?
It was sort of plane.

Which birds are best at construction?

Cranes!

How do you get a flower to stay put?
You planter.

What do you call a good-looking cat?
Purrty.

Why won't dogs wear slacks?
They prefer pants.

What happened when the jeans completely wore out?
They just faded away.

Why are mountains so good at poker?
They can bluff really well.

How can you tell when your jeans are tired?
They pant.

Why didn't the pin cushion recognize the needle?
It was wearing new threads.

When are your clothes the most tired?
When you wear them out.

How did the hammer do at diving off the high board?
He nailed it.

What do you call a sofa trying to catch a chair?
A chaise.

Why did the cloud have trouble remembering stuff?

It was kind of foggy!

Why didn't the magician do his show?

He didn't wand to!

Where do the birds come up with their ideas?
They hatch them.

What did the teeth think of the gum's plan?
He chewed on it for a while.

Why was the ox so mad?
The yoke was on him.

What does a fish say when the other fish were laughing?
What's so finny?

How did the lollipop get over its cold?
It licked it.

How do potato chips cool off?

They take a dip!

Where do big letters like to go on vacation?

To the capital.

Why do miners really like their jobs?

They really dig it!

How did the soldier get the job done right?

With a lot of attention!

Why do teeth have trouble making decisions?
They don't know what to chews.

What did the fog say when it missed the first time?
I can dew this!

How did the farmer look in his new clothes?
OK, overall.

How do evergreens stay warm?
They wear fir coats.

How do tiny insects get away?
They flea.

Why was the river so loud?

It had a big mouth!

How did the restaurant feel about so many guests?
It had some reservations.

Why was the flute so tired?
It had been carrying a tune.

Why are plumbers always so tired?
Their work is very draining.

Why did the comb go to the dentist?
To get its teeth cleaned.

Why did the police officer have to go to bed?
He needed arrest.

What do tightrope walkers eat?

Balanced diets!

Why are flowers so well-rested?
They're always in their beds.

Why was the package always getting into trouble?
It liked to box.

What day of the week is hardest on eggs?
Fryday.

Why can't jokes eat very fast?
They might gag.

Why couldn't they get the paste away from the TV?
It was glued to it.

What kind of tree has the most friends?

A poplar tree!

What kind of dogs do scientists have?
Labs.

How did the bolts get the nuts from place to place?
They lugged them around.

Why did the jam need more room?
It liked to spread out.

Why didn't anyone believe the blow dryer?
It was full of hot air.

Was the mower on time to the lawn's party?
Yes, but he cut it close.

How does a duck find what it
is looking for on the Internet?

It Gaggles it!

Why was the macaroni's mother so steamed?
His elbows were on the table.

What did the margarine say to the bread?
You butter not.

What happens if your eyes get too cold?
You get eye-sicles.

Why wouldn't the bulb light up?
It was a flower bulb.

What is soda's favorite game?
Follow the liter.

What do you get when cover your mattress with jam?
A bed spread.

Why was the shirt spinning around?
It was a top.

Why was the tennis ball covering its ears?
There was too much racket.

Why did the hammer go to the salon?
It wanted to have its nails done.

What did the trains do when it started to snow?
They froze in their tracks.

Why was the tree digging in the ground?
It was trying to find the root of the problem.

What happened when the bird flew through the car wash?

It got de-tailed!

What did the soda do with its frustration?

Kept it bottled up!

Why did the cars keep hitting the trees?
They were on the wrong root.

What is the big rock's favorite city?
Boulder.

What did the trees do when the wind came by?
They split.

Why wouldn't the sweater talk to the dryer?
It gave her too much static.

Where did the railroad's tie go?
The train kept track of it.

Who is the hungriest superhero of all?

Supperman!

What do superheroes do when things don't go their way?
POW-t.

Why doesn't Batman play cards?
He doesn't want anything to do with the Joker.

How did the parachutes get tricked?
They fell for it.

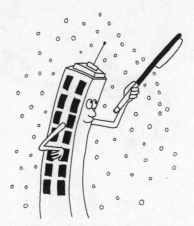

How do you get snow out of the air?

Use a skyscraper!

What do you get when you put one night above another?
An over nighter.

Why did the superhero save the chicken?
Because it tried to cross the road at rush hour.

What kind of beam can you never walk across?
A beam of light.

What do superheroes use to fix their ripped disguises?
Masking tape.

What did the sun say to the cloud?
I'm going to shine weather you like it or not.

Which superhero is the most curious?

Wonder Woman!

What did the rocket say to Earth?
I'm gonna have to take off now.

What did one mallard say to the other when a low-flying plane came by?
Duck!

Why did the rocket fall over?
It was a little off base.

What kind of bolt never needs a nut?
A lightning bolt.

Where did the mist go?
It vanished into thin air.

What did the cheese call the sandwich?

My hero.

Why was the sleet in bed?

It was under the weather.

How did Buzz do in space?

He went above and beyond.

How did the ocean keep its floor?

Very tidy.

How do galaxies work out?

On their ellipticals.

Why was the wind always poor?

It blew all of its money!

Which one of Santa's reindeer flies the highest?
Comet.

How does a barber trim a planet's hair?
Eclipse it.

Why did the galaxy fall apart?
It spiraled out of control.

Why did the door leave the ball game?
Someone knocked it out of the park.

Why was the sun getting richer?
Because of its raise.

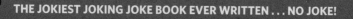

What did the sun say to the moon?

You're looking a little shady.

Why don't olives like being eaten?

It's the pits.

What do you call an old rocket?

A blast from the past.

What happens if you embarrass a planet?

It turns red.

What happens when the moon hits its head?

It sees stars.

Why did the spaceship miss the moon?

He didn't planet very well!

What did the rocket think of its ride?

It was a blast!

Where does the earth keep all of its trophies?
On its mantle.

What does the moon put its cheese on?
A crescent roll.

How does the North Star eat its ice cream?

With the Big Dipper!

How do stars get clean?
In meteor showers.

Why do planets have to clean all the time?
Because of the stardust.

What is an asteroid's favorite candy?
A fireball.

Why did the cups think they were in space?
The saucers were flying.

Why were the asteroids hiding from the comets?
They were tailing them.

Why was the
squirrel worried?

It went way out on a limb!

How do galaxies get really good reception?

From their satellites!

Why did the sun go to the eye doctor?
It was seeing spots.

How do asteroids keep their pants up?
With their belts.

What do pizza and the earth have in common?
Crust.

How do you know when a planet dies?
You read its orbituary.

How do you know when the planets are upset?
There's a revolution.

Who was the sorriest in the space program?

Apollo G!

Why did the sun think the planets were spacey?
They were a little far out there.

What did the moon say as it looked through the binoculars backwards?
What a small world.

How does the earth chop wood?
It uses its axis.

Why did the planet move to a bigger galaxy?
It needed more space.

What seems to always bring everyone down?
Gravity.

How do you know which is the moon's coat?
It has a silver lining.

How did the other planets learn the truth about the earth?
It surfaced.

Which cow gives the most milk?
The udder one.

What superhero is the hardest to find?
Wander woman.

What is a cloud's favorite sport?
Air hockey.

Where does Spiderman get his mail?

At his Web address!

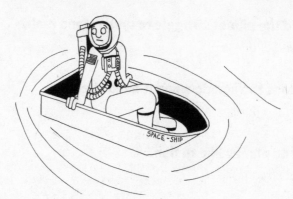

Why did the astronaut have to sit down in the boat?

He didn't want to rocket!

Why was the sun's birthday present wet?

It had a rain bow on it.

Who won in the race to the sun?

A passing cloud!

Why did the planet struggle to understand it all?
It was kind of dense.

What does the sun do when it needs help?
It sends up a flare.

Where do planes like to fish?
In the jet stream.

What sound does a shooting star make?
A big bang.

How did the earth catch two fish at once?
It used both of its poles.

What does the sun have when it sleeps?

Daydreams!

Why did the light get pulled over?

It was speeding.

What did the moon say about the ice cream cone?

It's out of this world.

Did you hear the story about the comet?

It's quite a tail.

What do stars get if they lose?

Constellation prizes.

How do you clean a black hole?

With a vacuum.

How did the cloud trick the lightning?

It stole its thunder!

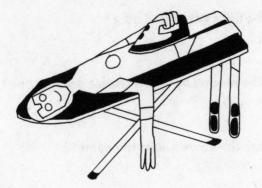

Who is the flattest superhero in the world?

Ironed man!

What kind of sound would the sky make if it was a lion?
Au-roar-a!

What is an astronaut's favorite dance?
The moonwalk.

Where do you go to buy a super hero?
A super market.

How do heroes keep it all together?
They use superglue.

What was the rope doing on the island?
It was stranded.

What do little rockets sit in?
Booster chairs.

What did the sun tell the moon when it was sad?
Look on the bright side.

What do a bathtub and Jupiter have in common?
Both of them have rings.

What kind of pets do stars have?
Sundogs.

Why was Mars so clean?
It was sun bathing.

Why was the cloud so rich?

It sold its silver lining!

What did the moon do when it grew up?

It went through a lot of phases!

How come the moon couldn't eat anymore?
Because it was full.

How can you tell when the moon is sad?
It's blue!

Why did the star looked so tired?
It was burnt out.

Where do they keep light when it's bad?
In prisms.

What was Walt Disney's favorite planet?
Pluto!

Where do Martians like to go for the summer?

Space camp!

How does the universe like its cereal?
The milky way.

How does Jupiter hold up its pants?
With an asteroid belt.

What's the moon's favorite gum?
Eclipse.

How does Neptune get clean?
With a meteor shower.

18
DEEP THOUGHTS

Why couldn't the bulb light up?

It had no ideas!

Why did everyone think the present was the smartest thing going?
It was gifted.

What do the words "behind," "tail," and "rear" have in common?
They are all back words.

Why did the fishing pole know all the answers?

It was a reel thinker.

What did the brain ask the machine?

M R I all right?

What do the North Pole and the South Pole have in common?

Nothing, they're polar opposites.

Why couldn't the skull think?

It was a no-brainer.

Why did the cauliflower struggle with putting the puzzle together?

It couldn't wrap its head around it.

Why wouldn't the duck fly away?

It was rubber!

Why did the cards have to quit the game?
Someone realized they weren't playing with a full deck.

Which kind of water has the most emotion?
The ocean, because it is so deep.

What kind of break doesn't hurt?
Spring break.

What has to go down before you can get up?
Your fever.

What do you get when you take the "hi" out of history?
Just another story.

Why was the egg so confused?

It was scrambled!

How can you make the word "gone" go away?
Put the word "all" in front of it.

How did the rope come untied?
They're knot sure.

How did the rhino let the other animals know they were in its way?
It used its horn.

What was the baby wearing on its face when it was born?
Nothing but a smile.

How many ways can you say the same thing?
One: "the same thing."

What did one brain ask the other?
What do you think?

What does one brain do when it sees another?
It waves.

In what ways can something last forever?
All-ways.

How do bridges handle things that get too deep?
They get over it.

Why did the ocean have to calm down?
It was making waves.

How did the magician make all of his problems go away?
With a little hocus pocus.

What season is the clumsiest?

Fall!

What do you call a tired snail?
Sluggish.

What do beds do when their work is all done?
They retire.

Why was the hair so upset?
Someone told a blonde joke.

Where can you find sad trash?
Down in the dumps.

What kitchen object is the sharpest?
The cleaver.

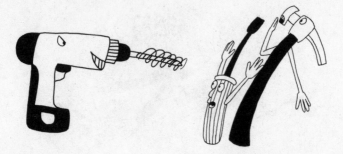

How did the power tool get the
answers it wanted from the other tools?

It drilled them!

What do skunks use to help themselves survive?
Their in-stinks.

What can be both hot and cold?
Chilly chili.

How come the hamper is only half full?
Somebody decided to clothes it.

Why did the bush think the tree was a dog?
Because of its bark.

Why couldn't the one joke stop laughing at the other?
It was too punny.

How did the tree make so many friends?

He branched out!

How do you know when a snowbank is totally lost?
It doesn't catch your drift.

How did the pond get so big?
Lake I know!

Why wouldn't the leaves go near the bonfire?
They were afraid someone might rake them over the coals.

How do you know the ground has given up?
It caves in.

Why did the doctor have to check on the well?
It looked a little pail.

Why did one shepherd walk on all fours?

He was acting kind of sheepish!

How did the tree store make so much money?
It branched out.

Why was the mirror so quiet?

It was reflecting on what had just happened!

Why couldn't the clown find his red rubber ball?

It was right in front of his nose!

Why weren't the eggs very fond of school?
They didn't like getting graded all the time.

Why did everyone think the egg was crazy?
It was cracking up.

How do you fix a broken fishing pole?
You put a cast on it.

Where do cards hang out in the summer?
On the deck.

How come the wave stopped moving?
Because it was tide up.

How does music communicate?

With notes!

Why does the weather always think it looks good?
Because it's a little vane.

Where do beauticians keep their clothes?

In hair dressers!

Why is the sponge always out in the sun?

It loves to soak it in!

What did the hotel tell the dog?
Stay.

What kind of dog wanders off the most?
A stray.

What time do most people eat?
At ate.

How do balls go from place to place?
They get around.

Why did it take so long to catch the swimsuit in its crime?
There was a cover up.

I heard there was an accident here?
Dent you know?

What is a tire's favorite hairstyle?

Treadlocks!

How did the artwork win a prize?
It entered a drawing.

Where do stoves get their ideas?
They cook them up.

Where do fish hold school?
In think tanks.

How did the lake ever make a decision?
By pondering it for a while.

Why did the arrow try for the job?
It wanted to shoot for its dreams.

How come the paper looked so old?

It was all wrinkled!

Why wouldn't the duck fly away?
It was rubber.

How did the book know what the brain was thinking?
It could read its mind.

What did the snowman do when the sun came out?
He had a meltdown.

Who did the judge call in the clothing case?
The material witness.

How do you clean a mind?
You brainwash it.

Why did the brain wish it was glass?

It wanted a clear conscience.

What kind of joke can never be told outdoors?

An inside joke.

What did the dancer think of having to do the same thing day after day?

It was a little too routine.

What did the mop say about forgetting the water on the floor?

It totally slipped my mind.

How did the yo-yo handle life's ups and downs?

It bounced back every time!

What do dentists do in the Army?

They're drill sergeants!

Did the tree ever solve the riddle?
No, it was stumped.

What happens when water drops?
It falls.

Why was the year concerned about the seasons?
They had changed.

What did the future never expect to see?
A present.

What do oceans sit on most of the time?
Their bottoms.

What is that smell?
Nobody nose.

What can be very quiet and last a long time?
The word still.

Why was the boy's head all cloudy?
Because he was brainstorming.

How come no one trusted the boa?
It was kind of snakey.

What happens when you mix salt and pepper?
A new flavor that is something to sneeze about.

Why was the sidewalk upset?
Everyone walked all over it.

How is the zipper doing?
It has its ups and downs.

Why couldn't the border make up its mind?
It was on the edge.

What did the taffy do when everything started coming apart?
They pulled it together.

Why couldn't the balloon go with the others?
It was a little deflated.

19
FUNNY BONE—Zombies, Skeletons, Ghosts, etc.

What kind of story would a ghostwriter write?
A spooky one.

What do you call it when a baby vampire crawls?
A little creepy.

Why do zombies walk so slow?
Because they're dead tired.

What do mad mops do?

Kick the bucket!

How do you know if you're a ghost?
When food goes right through you.

What do baby zombies wear?
Die-pers.

What do you call zombie phones?
Dead ringers.

How do you know when two zombies are talking?
It's dead quiet.

What do little spirits like before bed?
Ghost stories.

What does a ghost say when you knock at the door?
Boo is it?

How do you know when a poltergeist is scared?
He's white as a ghost.

How did the skeleton get in the house?
It used its key.

What do you say to a zombie without a brain?
Nevermind.

How can you be sure when a zombie isn't right?
When they're dead wrong.

What does a ghost call its favorite person?

My Boo!

Why couldn't the stone be a grave marker?
It couldn't get a head.

What did the skeleton think of the grave?
It was a little shallow at times.

What would happen if someone took everything out of the freezer?
Ice cream.

How did the glass know everything was going to be all right?
There was a light at the end of the funnel.

Why does it take longer for a two-headed monster to answer a question?
It has to think twice.

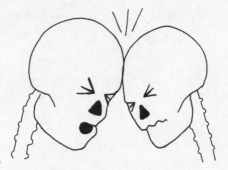

What do skeletons get
when they bump their heads?

Numbskulls!

How did the milk know its time had come?

It was ready to expire.

Why couldn't the skeleton laugh?

He was missing his funny bone.

What do you call someone with a hat made out of bones?

Bonehead.

Why did the zombie stop its car?

It reached a dead end.

Do zombies ever rest?

Of corpse they don't.

What do a bunch of ghosts playing baseball have?
Team spirit.

What is a skeleton's favorite part of Thanksgiving?
The wishbone.

What do ghosts read in their spare time?
Booooooooks.

How long was the rabbit gone?
The hole day.

Why were the skeletons shocked when they looked in the grave?
No body was there.

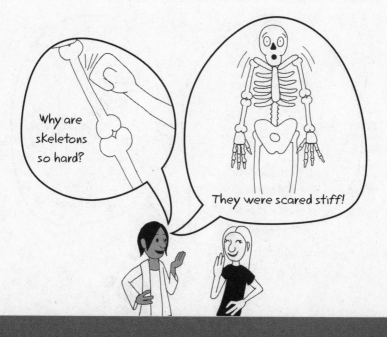

Why are skeletons so hard?

They were scared stiff!

How did all the colors become extinct?
They all dyed out.

What do you get when you cross a skeleton with a genie?
A wish bone.

What was the alphabet's favorite food?
Soup!

Why can't anyone sleep at a funeral?
Because it's a wake.

Was there any sign the candle was alive?
Just a flicker.

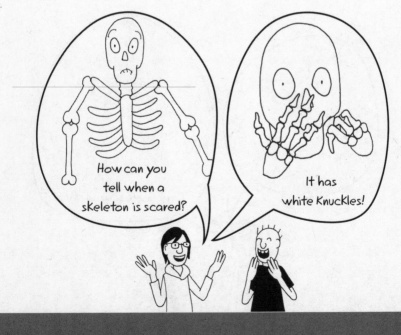

How can you tell when a skeleton is scared?

It has white Knuckles!

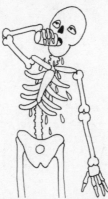

How can you tell when a skeleton needs a drink?

It's bone-dry!

Why was the broom confused?
It didn't know which witch was which.

How did the hair feel about being put in braids?
It dreaded it.

How did the power cord feel about seeing a ghost?
It was a shock.

Why was Frankenstein's monster such a good dresser?
He was always put together.

What did the bucket look like when it saw the ghost?
It was very pail.

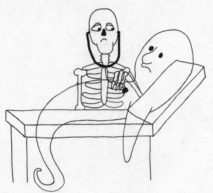

Why was the skeleton worried about the ghost?

He wasn't all there!

What is a ghost's favorite fruit?
Boo-berries!

How do you feel when you have lice?
Lousy.

What is a skeleton's favorite food?
Spare ribs.

What did the bunny think of the scary movie?
It was hare-raising.

Why wouldn't the wood go into the haunted house?
It was petrified.

What is a zombie's favorite time of the day?

Mourning!

Do cemetery workers like their job?

They dig it.

What did the snake do when it saw the ghost?
It jumped right out of its skin.

What happened when the vampire dropped his dinner?
He made a bloody mess.

How did the building know the ground was scared?
It was quaking.

Why were the two bears so different?
They were polar.

What were the turkeys so scared of?
The goblin'.

What did the windows do when they realized the house was haunted?

They shuttered!

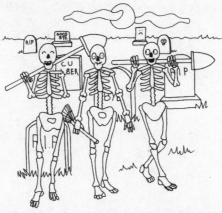

Who works the graveyard shift?

The skeleton crew!

Who did the crying ghoul want?
Its mummie.

How come nobody wanted to hang out with the vampire?
He was a pain in the neck.

Which subject are witches best at?
Spelling.

How come witches' hats make them so clever?
They get the point.

Who was the nose the most afraid of?
The boogie man.

Why do ghosts make the best cheerleaders?

They have the most spirit!

How come vampires are never late for dinner?

Because they're punctural.

Why was the skeleton dead tired?

He worked the graveyard shift!

How come nobody likes to have dinner with a vampire?

It's too draining.

What did the wolf ask the moon?

Howl we ever get there.

What did the zombie do when it walked into a ceiling fan?

It lost its head.

Why did everyone laugh at the werewolf?

He was a howl.

What did the water do that was so scary?

It roared.

Why were the Zombies in a hurry to go to the party?

They were dying to meet everyone!

What do you call a vampire rock concert?

A monster jam!

How did the ghost feel about the love of her life?
She was errie-sistible.

How did the witch put a curse on the hive?
With a spelling bee.

Why was the Wicked Witch sent to her room?
She had a meltdown.

What do you do with a hot ghost?
Phantom.

What did Frankenstein's monster think of his bolts?
They were a pain in the neck.

What did the skeleton tell
the sheets about their secret?

Mummies the word!

What do you call a really scared cow?
A Coward.

Why did the ghosts have to leave the ball game?
They were booing everyone.

What kind of shampoo does Medusa use?
Snake Heads and Shoulders.

What do you get when you cross a vampire with a beagle?
A bloodhound.

Why was the Minotaur so stubborn?
Because he was bullheaded.

Why are zombies such good workers?

They are very deadicated!

Who is the biggest horse fly?
Pegasus.

How does Bigfoot tell time?
With a Sasqwatch.

What did one unicorn say to the other?
I get the point.

Why was Frankenstein's monster so unhappy?
He had two left feet.

How do ghosts handle their problems?
They try to see through them.

THE JOKIEST JOKING JOKE BOOK EVER WRITTEN . . . NO JOKE!

How were things looking for the headstone?

Very grave!

How did Frankenstein's monster feel about his surgery?
He was scarred for life.

How can you tell when a leprechaun is jealous?
He's green with envy.

How come no one likes to listen to Puff's stories?
Because he would always drag on.

Why didn't anyone invite the Dementors to the party?
Because they sucked the life out of the room.

How come no one took the centaur seriously?
Because he was always horsing around.

What do you call it when electricity marries gas?

A power couple!

What did the hair do when it all fell out?
It bald.

What did the plank say after lying around all day?
I'm board.

What four letters can get you out of trouble?
HELP.

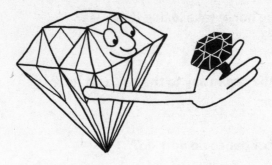

What did the diamond think of the ruby?

She was a real gem!

What did the letters say when the phone rang?
L, O.

How did the alphabet do on its tests?
It got an A, B, and a C.

What happens if U doesn't win?
U loses.

Which three letters make you hungry just thinking about them?
P, B, and J.

What did the paper say to the tape?
Let's wrap this up!

How did the horse take losing its shoes?
It felt defeeted.

What did the ocean say to the bay as it left?
Sea you soon.

What kind of dance do dots do?
The polka.

Why did the bird take a nap?
It needed a little down time.

What do cold geese get?
Goosebumps.

Why did the pan stop hanging around the plastic wrap?

It was too clingy!

What did the backpack tell the jogging shoes when they broke up?

Take a hike!

Why aren't robbers funny?
They can't take a joke.

What did the clock do for the dancer?
She gave him a big hand.

What did one buffalo say to the other buffaloes?
I herd you were coming to town!

Why did the eyes do so well in their business?
They were never closed.

How do you kiss a moth?
With butterfly kisses.

How do you know when a tub is married?
It has a ring.

What kind of boat never needs water?

A dreamboat!

What did the two ropes do at their wedding?
They tied the knot.

Who did the salad want to marry: the croutons or the dressing?
It was a toss-up.

How did it go for the pie and the cake?
They loved each other to pieces.

Why was the trash so hurt by the can?
She dumped him.

Why didn't the socks stay together?

They weren't a good match!

What did the two pieces of bread give each other on their first date?
A toast.

What does an aunt do if she can't get married?
Antelope.

Who are the most romantic of the fruits?
The dates.

What did the finger think of the thumb?
It was handsome.

How did the polish feel about the mop?
It took a shine to it.

Which is the most curious letter?

Y!

How could you tell the pickles were fond of one another?
The relished each other.

What did music say when the lyric asked if it would go out?
Of chords I will.

Who broke the dish's heart?
Someone named Chip.

What kind of couple did the lighter and the fluid make?
A perfect match.

Did you hear about the wall and the plaster not getting along?
They patched things up.

346   THE JOKIEST JOKING JOKE BOOK EVER WRITTEN . . . NO JOKE!

What do you get when you
put four quarters on a duck's beak?

A dollar bill!

What happened when the joke married the pun?
They lived happily ever laughter.

What did one period mean when it told the other it was over?
It was definitely the end.

Why wouldn't the sweet potatoes hang out with the regular spuds?
They just didn't mash up.

What did the match call the candle?
Her new flame.

What did the glass think of the window cleaner?
It took a shine to him.

Where did the two cows go on their first date?

To the mooovies!

What happened when the pecan and the almond met?

They were nuts about each other.

What happened when the boat lost the anchor?

It was grounded!

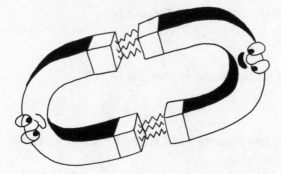

What did the one magnet think about the other?

It found it attractive!

How did one tunnel break up with the other?
We are through!

Was the battery sure she wanted to marry the other magnet?
Yes, she was positive.

What is something two lies can never have?
True love.

How did Jill fall?
Head over hills for Jack.

Why was the bracelet always so happy?
It had a charmed life.

What did the tree say to the bush?
Wood you like to go out?

Where did the calendar and prune go?
Out on a date.

What did the phones have when they got married?
An excellent reception.

What did the carrots say to the roast?
Nice to meat you.

What did one prisoner ask the other?
Are you free tonight?

How did the plug and the outlet
know they were meant to be together?

They had a real connection?

How did the mountains and the boulders get along?
It was a little rocky at first.

How did the water feel about the pan meeting up with the stove?
It was boiling mad.

Why did the yardstick break up with the ruler?
It didn't measure up.

What happened when the paper and the glue met?
They stayed together.

Why didn't the walls trust the ceiling?
It was up to no good.

What did the really long syringe think it was?
A big shot.

What happened between the two sticks of dynamite?
They had a blowup.

What happened when the boat lost the anchor?
Its heart sank.

Why did the wrapper fall in love with the candy bar?
Because it was so sweet.

What did the paper plate think of the china?
She was a real dish.

Why was the pepper so taken with the salt?

It was dashing!

What did the two candles do for fun?

They went out!

Why did everyone fall in love with the heart?
You just can't beat it.

Did you hear the one about the orange and the watermelon?
It's real juicy.

What kind of relationship did the heart and the monitor have?
Steady.

What happened to the two cars after a couple of dates?
They were going together.

What happened when the match and the fireworks went out?
There were lots of sparks.

How did the lion and the lioness feel?

They were wild about each other!

How do you keep a necklace safe?
You locket.

Why didn't the keyboard date the mouse?

He wasn't her type!

Why did the pot and the fork get together often?

They were fondue each other!

How did the two stars get along together?
Heavenly.

What did the pot holder think of the pan?
It was hot.

How did the blender feel about the ice?
It had a crush on it.

What did the two shades call their night out?
A blind date.

How did the pancake feel when the spatula asked it out?
It was flattered.

What was the relationship between
the clouds and the rain like?

It was a little stormy!

What did the laces tell the bow?
Forget-me-knot.

What do lightning and thunder call a night on the town?
A rain date.

What did the bee call the comb?
Honey.

What did the stag call his doe?
Dear.

What was the knife like on the first date?
A little dull.

How did the cake show the cookie it cared?

It gave her flours!

Why did the fruit trees get married?
They made quite a pear.

Where did the spider meet the fly?
On the Web.

What happened when the paint and the brush got together?
The wall got a new coat for winter.

What do flowers call their friends?
Their bud-dies.

Why didn't the stripes and the polka dots ever go out?
They clashed.